Alessandro Bizzozero | Richard McGrand | Boris Bartels

After Brexit

Alessandro Bizzozero
Richard McGrand
Boris Bartels

After Brexit

Cross-border financial services from the UK into the EU

brp
Bizzozero & Partners
Regulatory Products

Schulthess § 2017

Suggested quotation: ALESSANDRO BIZZOZERO/RICHARD MCGRAND/BORIS BARTELS, *After Brexit – Cross-border financial services from the UK into the EU*, Geneva/Zurich 2017, Schulthess

Bibliographic information published by the Deutsche Nationalbibliothek
The Deutsche Nationalbibliothek lists this publication in the Deutsche Nationalbibliografie; detailed bibliographic data are available in the Internet at http://dnb.d-nb.de.

ISBN 978-3-7255-8670-7

www.schulthess.com

Following the UK's decision to withdraw from the EU, UK financial services firms need to consider their future options for prospecting and conducting business in the remaining 27 EU countries. This paper covers the essential concepts related to financial cross-border activity and provides an overview of the obstacles to prospecting activities in EU Member States as well as local licensing constraints.

The paper looks at banking and investment services as well as product marketing and so should provide useful information to industry players, particularly in the event of a "hard" Brexit.

Table of Contents

List of Abbreviations

AIF	Alternative Investment Fund
AIFMD	Alternative Investment Fund Managers Directive
AML	Anti-money laundering
BaFin	Bundesanstalt für Finanzdienstleistungsaufsicht
Bull.	Bulletin
BVerwG	Bundesverwaltungsgericht
CCP	Central counterparty
CfD	Contract for difference
CFPG	Commissione ticinese per la formazione dei giuristi
CIS	Collective Investment Scheme
COM	European Commission
CONSOB	Commissione Nazionale per le Società e la Borsa
CMU	Capital Markets Union
CP	Consultation Paper
CRD	Capital Requirements Directive
CRR	Capital Requirements Regulation
CSMAD	Directive on criminal sanctions for insider dealing and market manipulation
CSSF	Commission de Surveillance du Secteur Financier
EBA	European Banking Authority
ECB	European Central Bank
EEA	European Economic Area
EEE	Espace Economique Européen
eIDAS regulation	regulation on electronic identification and trust services for electronic transactions in the internal market
EIOPA	European Insurance and Occupational Pensions Authority
ELTIF	European long-term investment fund
EMD	Electronic Money Directive
EMIR	European Market Infrastructure Regulation
ESA	European Supervisory Authority
ESMA	European Securities and Markets Authority
EU	European Union
EUCU	European Union Customs Union
EuSEF	European social entrepreneurship fund
EuVECA	European venture capital fund
FATF	Financial Action Task Force
FCA	Financial Conduct Authority
FINMA	Eidgenössische Finanzmarktaufsicht
FSMA	Autorité des services et marchés financiers
GATS	General agreement on trade in services
GDPR	General data protection regulation
HNWI	High net worth individual

IDD	Insurance Distribution Directive
IOSCO	International Organisation of Securities Commissions
KAGB	Kapitalanlagegesetzbuch
KID	Key information document
MAR	Market Abuse Regulation
MFSA	Malta Financial Services Authority
MiFID	Directive on markets in financial instruments
MiFIR	Regulation on markets in financial instruments
MMF	Money market fund
NPPR	National private placement regime
OECD	Organisation for economic cooperation and development
OJ	Official Journal of the EU
OLO	One-leg-out
PAD	Payment Accounts Directive
PD	Prospectus Directive
PEP	Politically exposed person
PRIIP	Packaged retail and insurance investment product
PS	Policy Statement
PSD	Payment Services Directive
Q&A	Question and answer
SEPA	Single European Payments Area
Seq.	subsequent
SFBC	Swiss Federal Banking Commission
STS securitisation	simple, transparent and standardised securitisation
UCITS	Undertakings for collective investment in transferable securities
UK	United Kingdom

Introduction

This paper covers two distinct activities: on the one hand, prospecting, i.e. any commercial practice related to promoting, selling or providing a service and, on the other hand, establishing business relationships[1], i.e. the conclusion of a contract for providing a service that may also involve investment in products. Our focus is entirely on the cross-border provision of services. This, however, will not prevent us from referring, occasionally, to regulations covering the promotion of financial products. By "financial services", we limit ourselves for discussion purposes to banking and investment services. The promotion of insurance services and products will not be covered. We will also not consider in detail the provision of financial services and resulting client reporting.

We will, however, cover prospecting and consequent steps taken by a UK financial services provider, ranging from advertising to direct or indirect contact with the client and to the conclusion of a contract. We will in particular focus on activities directed towards the EU and will look at the situation where UK financial services firms are unable to make use of European passports, i.e. the UK as a third country in relation to the EU. We will highlight the current legal and regulatory reality which UK financial services providers must take into account when deciding to enter the EU single market. The approach chosen goes beyond licensing requirements, even if these constraints will be subject to specific analysis. We intend to provide a broader view of the barriers that despite appearances may make access to the EU market more difficult than is currently perceived – even when using a passport.

After introducing the specific and so far unprecedented case of a major country such as the UK leaving the EU (Part 1), we will present the essential concepts related to financial cross-border activity (Part 2), provide an overview of the obstacles to prospecting activities directed towards EU Member States (Part 3). Finally, we will describe the particularities of the main constraint – obtaining a licence – in certain cases (Part 4).

---

1 Definition derived from art. 2(d) Directive 2005/29/EC of the European Parliament and of the Council of 11 May 2005 concerning unfair business-to-consumer commercial practices in the internal market, OJ L 149 dated 11 June 2005, p. 22.

Part 1:
UK's decision to leave the EU - Brexit

Following the 2016 referendum on continued membership the UK is now committed to leaving the EU. The UK government has passed legislation to invoke Article 50 of the Lisbon Treaty and formally initiated the process of leaving the EU by the exercise of Article 50 on 29th March 2017.

It seems that, subject to possible amendments and negotiations, the UK is aiming for a so called "hard" Brexit whereby it will neither retain membership of the European Economic Area nor remain in the EU Customs Union ("EUCU"). There remains the possibility that the UK will re-join the European Free Trade Association. It is likely that there may be some bilateral agreements in future between the UK and EU covering certain sectors of the economy. In particular, it would seem to be in the interests of both the EU and UK to make arrangements covering financial services which would cover transitional arrangements after the formal end of EU membership and if possible recognise mutual regulatory equivalence or adequacy. It does not seem likely that such arrangements would allow the flexibility or scope currently available under EU passporting arrangements.

The status of the various Crown dependencies following Brexit must also be mentioned. The Channel Islands (Jersey, Guernsey, Alderney and Sark) are not part of the UK but are Crown Dependencies. As such they are not in the EU or EEA and so already have third country status. The Isle of Man is in the same position. The financial services sector on each island appears comfortable with this and has tended to implement some EU equivalent measures via bilateral agreements in key areas such as investment funds to enable access to the EU market. Note, however that these islands are part of the EUCU so that their status with respect to import and export tariffs is unclear going forward.

Gibraltar in contrast is incorporated into the EU by virtue of the UK's membership. Therefore, when the UK leaves the EU so will Gibraltar and this could affect key sectors of the Gibraltarian financial services sector such as insurance. Interestingly Gibraltar is excluded from the EUCU. It is too early to say what the status of Gibraltar will be in the future – the picture is complicated by the troubled relationship with Spain which claims sovereignty. The Gibraltarians voted overwhelmingly to remain in the EU, but have also in the past voted overwhelmingly to remain a part of the UK.

Part 2:
Financial cross-border activity

When dealing with cross-border activity, in order to avoid any misunderstandings, it is always important to define such activity (Section A) and understand its scope with regard to the topic under discussion so that any necessary distinctions may be drawn (Section B).

Section A:
General definition and scope of financial cross-border activity

After defining cross-border activities (Chapter 1), we will detail the geographical scope of the concept (Chapter 2). In this context it is necessary to describe the problem of the extraterritorial scope of regulation (Chapter 3) and the threshold of tolerance of its application (Chapter 4).

Chapter 1: Definition

At a general level, cross-border activity may be defined as a "financial activity related to the export of services, the sale of a product abroad or an investment on a foreign regulated market"[2]. As mentioned in the introduction, we will only discuss the first one of these three activities, namely the export of financial services.

In itself, the cross-border activity of promoting a financial service can take various forms. The aim is always to promote and to sell a service to a person abroad (in the case of this paper a person present or resident/domiciled in an EU Member State). This is known as "export of services". As usually described in international agreements (e.g. GATS), four modes of exporting financial services are usually distinguished[3]: exporting a service through the establishment of an office in a target country (branch or representative office), exporting through prospecting or by providing services on-site without establishing any offices, exporting through prospecting or by providing services via remote means of communication from the head office of the service provider, and presenting services to a client resident in a target country who has travelled to the country of the service provider. In the following pages, we will concentrate on the last three modes of exporting, as the creation of an office is a subject in itself. A target country's financial regulation applicable to all three cross-border situations would have an absolute extraterritorial effect while regulation which applies only when the representative of the foreign financial firm is travelling on the target country's territory has a limited extraterritorial effect.

---

2 Bizzozero Alessandro/Robinson Christopher, Financial cross-border activities into and out of Switzerland, Fribourg, 2010, p. 26.

3 For more details, see: Bizzozero Alessandro/Robinson Christopher op. cit. p. 29 ff.

Chapter 2: Geographical scope of the concept

The scope of cross-border activity when promoting services directed towards the EU is a special case:

- With regard to the EU, there are two types of regulatory border. The first is that which exists as a political reality with a supranational regulatory body, common to the current 28 Member States. This is known as EU law. The second is the one resulting from the legal order of each Member State. This is known as national law. As we shall see in greater detail below, each Member State has legislative autonomy with regard to services that are not yet regulated at the EU level. This autonomy also exists, partially, within fields regulated at the EU level. This is in particular the case for banking and investment services. Any cross-border prospecting activity out of the UK towards the EU must therefore be examined both from an EU law and national law perspective.
- The concept of border does not refer to the political border, but to the border between different legal regimes. There is generally no cross-border activity between countries that have an identical and common legal order with a single regulator. Within the EU itself, this scenario does not occur - the closest parallel is the Monegasque situation. The Principality of Monaco, even though it is situated outside of the EU, applies French law to the provision of banking services, under the sole responsibility of the French regulator[4]. Despite this common identity between regulation and regulator, the jurisdictions have two different legal systems, as the agreements that bind them do not seem to envisage territorial unity regarding the provision of these services. On the other hand, if the same state has several financial legal systems, its political unity is not particularly relevant. An important example is certainly China, in relation to the territories of Hong Kong and Macao. These are three different and autonomous financial legal systems with three distinct regulators, even though they belong to a single state. UK service providers who intend to prospect in these territories must take into account the three regimes, depending on where they are prospecting and the residence of the client. There are other cases such as the United Arab Emirates, Qatar and Malaysia where there are various autonomous financial territories in each country.
- Under the British Crown there are the Crown dependencies (Jersey, Guernsey, Isle of Man) and the numerous Overseas Territories (which include Gibraltar). All these dependencies have their own financial legal system and their own regulators. Unlike Jersey, Guernsey and the Isle of Man, Gibraltar is part of the EU[5]. Within the EU and before the UK's EU membership termination will be effective, there are thus 29 legal systems, one more than the current number of Member States. Any cross-border

---

[4] On the exchange of letters between French and Monegasque authorities, see Bizzozero Alessandro/Robinson Christopher, op.cit. p. 64 f.

[5] Declaration n° 55 annexed to the Treaty on the FEU, OJ C 236, 26 October 2012, p. 47.

activity directed towards the EU must therefore take into account an additional legal system compared to the number of Member States.

- Cross-border activity is a factual concept that takes into account the residence or in some cases the residence/domicile of the prospect, the client or of the representative of the prospect/client, as well as their geographical location The nationality of these persons is not generally in itself a key element. There are, however, some exceptions. From a regulatory point of view, it is worthwhile mentioning Indonesia, where regulations on investment of products take into account the Indonesian nationality of an investor, irrespective of his location[6]. Thus, a product is subject to a prospectus which must be duly notified to the Indonesian authorities, if it is distributed annually to more than 100 potential investors of Indonesian nationality or to persons who live in Indonesia over the course of a year. At the EU level, what matters is always residency/domicile and the place where a financial services activity occurs or takes effect. An example can be found in Art. 42 of the Directive 2014/65/EU of the European Parliament and Council of 15 May 2014 on markets in financial instruments (hereafter MiFID II)[7], which, referring to the concept of reverse solicitation, explicitly mentions clients who are "*established* or *situated* in the EU".

It must also be remembered that EU law on financial services goes beyond the EU and extends to the European Economic Area (hereafter EEA)[8]. The considerations expressed in this paper thus also apply to those non-Member States of the EU (Liechtenstein, Norway and Iceland) that have joined the EEA.

Chapter 3: Extraterritorial impact

Cross-border activity confronts a foreign financial services provider with regulations that are different from those of its country of incorporation. These rules have an extraterritorial impact if the foreign service provider is required to comply with them. The stronger the link with the foreign country, the higher the risk of an extraterritorial impact. However, this impact can even exist when prospecting and where the execution of a service take place in the provider's and not the client's country.

In the financial field, EU law and the national law of Member States often have an extraterritorial impact. This varies considerably depending on the service or product offered. The strongest extraterritorial impact derives from EU or national rules regarding the offer of financial products. A significant example is the Directive on Alternative Investment Fund Managers (hereafter AIFMD)[9]. According to this directive, offering alternative investment funds can even be problematic if an EU investor is located in a non-EU country such as Switzerland when he receives information. AIFMD restrictions have to be taken into account

---

6 Art. 1(15) Capital Market Law N° 8, 1995.

7 OJ L 173, 12 June 2014, p. 349.

8 Agreement on the European Economic Area.

9 Directive 2011/61/EU of the European Parliament and of the Council of 8 June 2011 on alternative investment fund managers, OJ L 174, 1 July 2011, p. 1.

by third-country managers. German national regulations reinforce this effect by (subject to certain exceptions) prohibiting the placement of non-authorised products in portfolios of German managed clients, regardless of whether the portfolio is managed in Germany or elsewhere[10].

There is a different approach for UCITS[11] funds as opposed to AIFs: a UCITS fund established in an EU member State may be offered to a person in another Member State if said fund has been notified in the target EU State. Third-country funds are not mentioned at all. It must be remembered, however that even when marketing an EU UCITS within the EU, different countries have different approaches as to what constitutes marketing and residency and other variable criteria may apply.

Chapter 4: Criteria of attraction and threshold of tolerance

To understand the cross-border regime of a target country towards foreign financial intermediaries, the regulatory situation should be assessed based on the following steps:

4.1 Criteria of attraction

Where a UK financial services entity has established a permanent presence in an EU country local regulatory standards apply to any regulated activity conducted by that office and so a license would be required in the absence of a passport. For prospecting and services conducted in an EU country without a permanent presence the impact of the country's licensing, conduct and other regulatory provisions depends on the criterion of application in relation to local law and also the threshold of tolerance.

It is very common for countries to apply a criterion of territoriality, i.e. there is a link between activity and the territory of a country. A link may only be created if there is physical presence in the target country, but could also occur where there is communication by remote means. There are various approaches adopted by EU countries, for example:

> in Italy solicitation in relation to investment services directed at Italy triggers the application of Italian law regardless of the location where it is initiated and if a firm contacts an Italian resident by telephone from abroad this may be deemed to constitute solicitation if the purpose of the call is to present or propose a product or a service. This approach seems likely to change following the implementation of the MiFID II package;

[10] BaFin, Häufige Fragen zum Vertrieb und Erwerb von Investmentvermögen nach dem KAGB, WA 41-Wp 2137-2013/0293, 4 July 2013 and 20 March 2015.

[11] Undertakings for collective investment in transferable securities based on the UCITS Directive, Directive 2009/65/EC of the European Parliament and of the Council of 13 July 2009 on the coordination of laws, regulations and administrative provisions relating to undertakings for collective investment in transferable securities (UCITS), OJ L 302, 17 November 2009, p. 32.

> in Austria any territorial connection must be considered with regard to the overall circumstances.

Instead of applying a territorial criterion certain other non-EU countries apply residency based criteria, i.e. linked to the person. The USA and Canada are notable in this respect for investment services. The same occurs in South Korea and in Japan where a UK investment firm could be within the scope of local regulation and need a local licence just because it has clients resident in one of these countries.

4.2 Threshold of tolerance

Where a country has adopted a territorial criterion the application of that country's law and regulation depends on its interpretation of when a service is provided. In many countries a **solicitation test** is relevant so that local law applies as soon as a foreign entity markets its services or advertises or enters into discussions with prospects. France, Belgium, Germany. Italy and Austria are all EU countries that use a solicitation test.

Other countries prefer the more liberal **performance test** so that the law only applies to a service provided on a country's territory. The characteristic performance test has been endorsed by the European Commission and applies to the place of essential supply of the service for which payment is due. This is applied by the UK and others, at least for some financial services.

Finally, the most liberal threshold is the **lasting presence test**. This test applies national law only if individuals authorised to provide financial services or able to contract on behalf of a foreign financial institution are active within the territory of the country in question. So in practice local law tends only to apply to a permanent or well established presence in the country. Switzerland adopts this approach, although this may change, as do Russia and Armenia.

4.3 Safe harbours

Once the regulatory situation and any extraterritorial impact is understood for a particular country, it is imperative to check if local regulation grants any safe harbours. For instance, there may be exceptions and/or special regimes depending on the status of the investor or the level of prospecting activity.

Section B:
Distinctions

To gain a better understanding of the regulatory approach regarding the activity of prospecting into the EU, it is useful to highlight the following distinctions[12].

Chapter 1: Direct and indirect prospecting

First of all, one must differentiate between direct and indirect cross-border activity. An activity is direct when a financial service provider acts directly through its employees or its bodies. Indirect activity is when a company acts through a third party. For the prospecting phase, the provider may conclude contracts with finders or introducers. In any case, the activity carried out is normally linked to the service provider[13].

Engaging third parties is not a wholly viable solution to circumvent the obstacles that limit access to the EU market. The operational framework of the third party is subject to the same regulatory restrictions that apply to any direct activity and which vary according to each Member State. A restrictive country will only tolerate limited use of introducers. As an example, the Italian regulator accepts that banks use *segnalatori di pregi*, i.e. persons who can only indicate the existence of foreign service providers, but who are not authorised to promote their activity. Thus, these persons can only act within the same limits as the service providers themselves.

Similarly engaging third parties is not a solution to avoid constraints applied by rules on investor and consumer protection. These protections remain in place. In addition, EU rules on inducements may also apply.

Under certain EU Directives there is a concept of a tied agent (for example, in MiFID, the Insurance Mediation/Distribution Directive and the Payment Services Directive). The use of a tied agent in a particular country effectively leads to an establishment in that country.

Under MiFID a tied agent is defined (Art 4(1)(25)) as a "a person who, under the full and unconditional responsibility of only one MiFID investment firm or third country investment firm on whose behalf it acts, promotes investment services and/or ancillary services to clients or prospective clients, receives and transmits instructions or orders from the client in respect of investment services or financial instruments, places financial instruments and/or provides advice to clients or prospective clients in respect of those financial instruments or investment services". Where the tied agent is located in another EEA member state from the home state of the MiFID investment firms this would need to be notified under the right of establishment. The tied agent is restricted in what activities it can conduct as per the

[12] For more details, see Bizzozero Alessandro/Robinson Christopher op. cit., p.33 ff.

[13] On this subject, see Bizzozero Alessandro / Maillard Sophie, Gérants indépendants – Gestion des risques par la banque dépositaire, Geneva (Schulthess), 2014, p. 50 ff.

definition above and Article 23 of MiFID. The tied agent can only passport under the rights of the principal, it cannot passport in its own right. Under MiFID II there are some relatively minor changes to the tied agents regime, but it is notable that it will be mandatory across all EU member states.

Chapter 2: Active and passive prospecting

The active or passive character of prospecting depends upon the initiator of this activity. Prospecting is active (i.e. on an unsolicited basis), if it is initiated by the service provider, and it is passive (i.e. solicited) if it is initiated by the prospect or the client The passive approach is often referred to as reverse solicitation or reverse enquiry. In order to determine who the initiator is, there is a concept of an "initiative test".

The distinction between active and passive prospecting is essential when considering cross-border activity towards EU countries. The legal regime and consequently the operational possibilities can vary significantly according to the type of prospecting. When a foreign firm acts following a prospect's initiative, it often avoids the application of regulations covering the promotion of services. This theme will be developed below under IV.B.2.

Part 3:
General overview of obstacles to financial cross-border activity

Although barriers to the penetration of foreign markets have existed for a long time, they have been highlighted by the experience of Swiss banks following the UBS affair in the USA[14]. Historically, those financial institutions engaged in cross-border activity did not sufficiently focus their attention on regulatory limitations on access to foreign markets. Now an in-depth analysis of the legal framework must take other aspects into account. The obstacles to market access can thus arise from different sources. In this Part 3, we present the main obstacles encountered when prospecting and establishing business relationships and examine whether these are relevant for activities directed towards the EU from the UK. We follow the sequence shown in the table below. The regulatory barrier of licensing will then be discussed in more detail in Part 4.

In chronological order with regard to prospecting activity, barriers can be summarised in the graphic below:

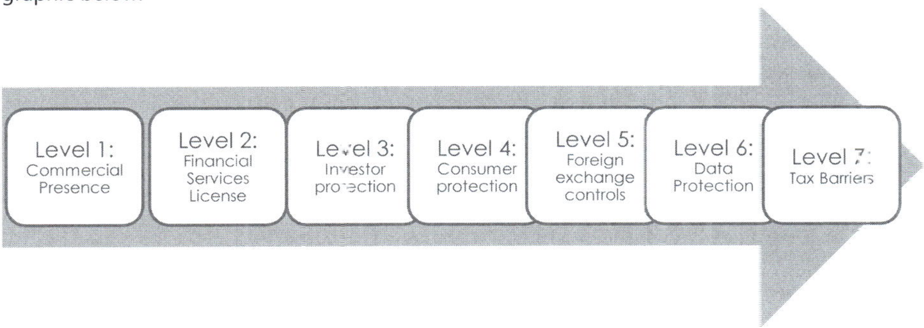

Section A:
Obstacles due to commercial law

The first limitation that must be taken account of when targeting a foreign market is the general requirement that exists in certain countries to enter a commercial presence in a commercial register or to obtain a commercial licence when carrying out a commercial activity on national territory or when promoting such an activity. This requirement concerns financial, but also other types of commercial and industrial activities. However, it does not concern activities carried out via remote means of communication from the country of the provider into the target country.

[14] Regarding the procedure against UBS, see in particular SFBC Annual Report 2008, p. 38. On the history of FINMA's interventions regarding cross-border activity, see in particular Bizzozero Alessandro, *Obligations cross-border pour une banque de gestion de fortune* in "La responsibilità in ambito bancario e nella gestione patrimoniale", CFPG Bull. N.47, Bellinzona 2012, 128 ff.

The registration requirement constitutes an obstacle to undertaking financial services activity only in so far as it is more stringent than any regulatory licence requirement resulting from financial services laws. For example, a UK firm could promote its financial services on-site without obtaining a licence, but in certain countries would not be able to do this without registering a branch in the local registry. Of course, the duty to register entails, for financial services firms, a *de facto* requirement to also obtain authorisation from the supervisory authorities of the financial sector, without which it would not be possible to register a branch. The consequences of breaching this registration requirement are sometimes only administrative, but could be criminal.

On the European continent, the best-known example is the Principality of Monaco[15]. Here, the provision of services on-site requires registration of a commercial presence. Outside of Europe, Bolivia[16] in the Americas and New Zealand for Oceania[17] can be mentioned. As for EU Member States, the general requirement to register commercial activity is not a significant obstacle, as it is preceded by the regulatory requirement to obtain a licence from a supervisory authority.

Section B:
Obstacles due to licensing restrictions

The obstacles as regards licensing restrictions must distinguish between services (Chapter 1) and products (Chapter 2).

Chapter 1: Licences restrictions on services

1.1. General principles

The second obstacle to the promotion of financial services directed towards a target country is the requirement to obtain a licence from the authorities of that country if the activity falls within the scope of application of local financial services laws. This is obviously the main restriction on cross-border activity. For assessing the regulatory situation of the target country, a legal analyses should be made based on the already mentioned three steps criteria of attraction, threshold of tolerance and safe harbour (see Part 2.A.4).

The requirement to obtain a licence varies according to national laws. There are, for example, liberal countries that authorise promotional activities from abroad or on-site without having to obtain a licence. Under such regimes, compliance with financial services laws is only necessary when contracts are signed on national territory, when a bank provides services

15 Law 1.144, 26/7/1991 on exercising certain economic and legal activities. This law imposes administrative authorisation, under penalty of administrative measures and criminal sanctions.

16 Art. 415, Code of Commerce.

17 Chap. 18, Company Act.

under a contract or when the bank's representatives stay in the country for a long period of time. Conversely, there are restrictive countries where any prospecting on-site, or even from abroad is subject to obtaining a licence. Sometimes, a licence is required even though the activity is entirely performed without any link to a third country, simply because the client is resident in this country. A UK firm would thus also need to have a licence if a client resident in the third country comes to the UK to receive a financial service. Such countries have a personal, not a territorial criterion of attraction. Relevant examples are few in number and typically only affect certain investment activities, to the exclusion of banking activities (Japan, South Korea, South Africa, Canada and, by extension of the concept of remote means of communication, the USA[18]). At the European level, only the AIFMD (and partially also the UCITS Directive) seem to follow a personal approach regarding the distribution of collective investments. As we have seen above, alternative investment funds must be registered in the investor's country of residence even if they are promoted from outside of the EU.

1.2. Types of licenses

Licences vary with regard to their nature and content:

- With regard to nature, one distinguishes between licences authorising a presence (subsidiary, branch and representative office) and licences available without a physical presence, generally known as cross-border licences. The latter are more interesting than the former as they avoid setting up expensive structures. Cross-border licences are assimilated to the exceptions to licensing that a foreign regulator can grant a firm in a third-country. In addition to the European countries that are mentioned below, there are other legal systems that offer this opportunity, in particular: Canada and the USA for the American continent; South Korea, Israel and Malaysia (personal licence), and India (in relation to remittance programs) for the Asian continent[19]. At the international level, cross-border licences are recognised by Article 2 of the Code of Liberalisation of Capital Movements and of Current Invisible Operations of the Organisation for Economic Co-operation (hereafter OECD)[20]. Their removal by a Member State of the OECD could constitute a breach of this agreement.
- With regard to their content, it should only be noted that the licence may have a general scope and authorise any type of banking or investment activity (universal licence e.g. Switzerland) or, on the contrary indicate in detail which activities the holder of the authorisation may carry out (e.g. the UK). At the EU level, Article 5 of MiFID II requires that Member States specify in their authorisation records which investment services a licensed company may provide.

---

18 On this matter see: Bizzozero Alessandro/Robinson Christopher, op.cit., p. 185 ff. Regarding the references mentioned in this paper, it should be noted that in 2015 South Africa amended the Financial Advisory and Investment Securities Act of 2002. The personal approach has been maintained and Chapter 1 now specifies that financial planning is part of the advisory activity, which is subject to authorisation.

19 For more details see: Bizzozero Alessandro/Robinson Christopher, op.cit. p. 211 ff.

20 The last version of the Code dated 2013 (www.oecd.org).

Operating without a licence may result in administrative measures and, not infrequently, in criminal sanctions[21].

1.3. Situation in the EU

The situation regarding licensing of financial activities in the EU must distinguish between banking (including payment) services on the one hand and investment services on the other. We will describe this in more detail in Part 4.

Chapter 2: Licences restrictions on products

2.1. General principles

The distribution of products regularly leads to the question whether the distribution activity signifies an investment service requiring authorisation, as well as whether the product itself requires local registration or notification. Financial products such as collective investment schemes and certain other products usually must be registered or notified. Furthermore, the bank distributing such products has to provide the investor with a prospectus and in specific cases also with other key investor information documents. Normally the approach seems to be a personal one depending on the residency of the investor and the regulation of the investor's country of residence might be applicable.[22]

2.2. Situation in the EU

The situation regarding licensing of financial products in the EU mainly distinguishes between transferable securities and the related prospectus requirements on the one hand and various kinds of investment funds on the other. We will describe this in more detail in Part 4.

Section C:
Obstacles due to investor protection

Investor protection is one of the main concerns of regulators and legislators. The first step is to put in place a licensing regime governing the provision of financial services activities. In addition to the licence, regulators can provide for conduct rules to preserve the interests of investors in their relationship with the service provider. Assuming that a UK firm can prospect in the target country, it therefore must ask itself whether there are any rules that define its activity (*how* to prospect and subsequently provide services). The complexity and the impact

[21] An example is art. 125, The Banking Act of the Republic of China, 24 June 2015 (Taiwan), which imposes a fine as well as custodial sentence from three to ten years for exercising a banking activity without authorisation.

[22] For more details see: Bizzozero Alessandro/Robinson Christopher, op.cit. p. 259 ff.

of these rules could have a deterrent effect and thus constitute a de facto obstacle to penetrating the foreign market.

Chapter 1: EU and local rules on investor protection

In the EU, protection of persons who invest in financial instruments or who receive investment services, is principally secured by MiFID and from 2018 its successor MiFID II. At the promotional level, the rules of conduct are defined in Articles 24 et seq. They relate in particular to the quality of information, including advertising and the suitability of proposed products. For insurance products, the Insurance Mediation Directive (Directive 2002/92/EC) and its successor, the Insurance Distribution Directive (Directive (EU) 2016/97), applicable as of 23 February 2018, contain similar provisions. We shall not go into the details of these requirements or lower level requirements.

Other EU law is also designed to protect the investor. Thus, Directive 2002/65/EC of the European Parliament and of the Council of 23 September 2002 concerning the distance marketing of consumer financial services[23] defines conduct rules with regard to establishing remote contact with the purpose of selling "any service of a banking, credit, insurance, personal pension, investment or payment nature" (Art. 2(b)). The prospect receives information on the supplier, the financial service and the content of the contract (Art. 3). This directive also grants clients a right of withdrawal (Art.6) and prohibits, without the investor's prior consent, certain unsolicited communications (Art. 10). The client must also be clearly informed of the language of communication and of the contract. This directive only applies to distance marketing wholly within the EU. A third-country firm would be subject to national implementation of this directive and any further local requirements applied at the national level which could fall under investor protection or consumer protection.

The content of information on financial products is governed by specific legislative acts which primarily serve the purpose of investor protection, in particular the Prospectus Directive and Regulation No 1286/2014 of the European Parliament and of the Council of 26 November 2014 on key information documents for packaged retail and insurance-based investment products (the PRIIPs Regulation[24]). The PRIIPs Regulation requires product manufacturers and distributors to provide retail investors with a key information document (KID) as pre-contractual information thus directly and indirectly affecting the promotion of PRIIPs towards EU clients. For example, a third-country manufacturer which cooperates with an EU distributor must relatively precisely determine the intended target market for the product and must deliver the information necessary to produce the KID.

---

23 OJ L 271, 9 October 2002, p.16.

24 OJ L 352, 9 December 2014, p.1; see also Commission Delegated Regulation (EU) 2017/653 of 8 March 2017 (...) laying down regulatory technical standards with regard to the presentation, content, review and revision of key information documents and the conditions for fulfilling the requirement to provide such documents, OJ L 100, 12 April 2017, p.1.

National transpositions and the additional rules that certain Member States have adopted, in particular those related to promotion, are also of interest. Italian legislation imposes specific door to door (*fuori sede* or *porta a porta)* rules for retail clients, which require having recourse to local advisors *(promotor finanziari)*[25]. Similar rules exist in other countries such as France or Belgium. Insofar as they apply to foreign banks that are active in these countries, these rules can complicate or even hinder any promotion. Such national rules can also apply to EU firms that operate in countries under the freedom to provide services as the concept of the general good permits such national restrictions. So even if UK firms were able to continue to utilise a passport after Brexit they would still have to take account of these rules.

Chapter 2: Applicability

In the absence of any established case-law or clear practice of local regulators, it is often difficult to determine the point at which these rules apply to a UK firm's prospecting activity in a Member State. We nevertheless think that they should and would apply in the following situations[26] :

> If a UK service provider has obtained a cross-border licence in the target country. This licence often makes foreign firms subject to conduct rules covering investor protection. This is in particular the case for prospecting rules in Italy and for Danish and Luxembourg laws on investor protection.
> The UK service provider breaches cross-border rules i.e. it operates without a licence although authorisation is required for activity conducted. This activity corresponds to a factual branch in the country, which is subject to investor protection regulation.
> The service provider openly directs his activity towards the investor's country[27].
> Where a UK service provider has established a permanent establishment in the target country. Local conduct requirements apply to both passported branches from EEA countries and third country branches in an EU member

In certain cases, however, there is absolute applicability of protection standards. The prospecting rules in France and other "règles de police", for example, apply under all circumstances[28].

---

25 Art. 79, Regolamento della CONSOB recante norme di autorizzazione del decreto legislative n. 58.

26 See also Bizzozero Alessandro, *Obligations cross-border pour une banque de gestion de* fortune in "La responsibilità in ambito bancario e nella gestione patrimoniale", CFPG Bull. N.47, Bellinzona 2012, 128 ff.

27 By analogy with Art. 6, Regulation n° 593/2008 of the European Parliament and of the Council of 17 June 2008 on the law applicable to contractual obligations (Rome I).

28 On this subject see SANBAR Wadie/BOUCHETEMBLE Hugues, Droit des opérations bancaires et financières transfrontalières – Aspects juridiques et pratiques de l'accès au marché français, Paris (RB édition), 2013.

Section D:
Obstacles due to consumer protection

Consumer protection provisions are another obstacle with wide ranging application and are sometimes linked to investor protection measures. They generally cover any commercial activity. Again, the purpose here is to understand *how* the UK service provider should act during the prospecting stage and when establishing a relationship, assuming that he does so within the operational limits permitted by local consumer and financial services regulation.

Depending on the content of these rules, their applicability and the legal consequences of any infringement, one cannot exclude that they constitute, in certain cases, a major obstacle to access to a national market or at least an element that in a peremptory manner would determine means of access. Note that failure to adhere to consumer protection requirements can lead to contracts being declared void in certain European countries; Belgium[29] is an example. Outside the EU, one could mention in particular the requirement to present all contracts in the local language if the client is a resident in Indonesia[30], failing which the contracts would be void[31]. Another example is the very strict regulation in Ghana regarding contact with a prospect via electronic means on an unsolicited basis[32].

Chapter 1: EU and local rules on consumer protection

Directive 2006/114/EC of the European Parliament and of the Council of 12 December 2006 concerning misleading and comparative advertising[33], even though it seeks to protect professionals and not consumers, imposes general constraints regarding advertising. Other EU regulation aims, in a more targeted way, to protect consumers of credit products. In addition to Directive 2014/17/EU of the European Parliament and of the Council of 4 February 2014 on credit agreements for consumers relating to residential immovable property (hereafter: the Mortgage Credit Directive)[34], governing real estate loans, reference should also be made to Directive 2008/48/EC of European Parliament and of the Council of 23 April 2008 on credit agreements for consumers (hereafter: the Consumer Credit Directive)[35], whose scope of application also includes small loans secured on security portfolios. This directive imposes minimum content requirements for all advertising communications and a duty to provide pre-contractual information[36].

---

29 See in particular Livres XI and XV, Code de droit économique.

30 Law N° 24 of 2009 on the National Flag, Language, Emblem and Anthem as well as Government Regulation N° 57 of 2014 on Development, Guidelines and Protection of Language and Literature.

31 West Jakarta District Decision N° 451/Pdt.G/2012/PN.Jkt.Bar on credit.

32 Section 50(5) of the Electronic Transaction Act, which prohibits any unsolicited electronic communication under penalty of a fine or a custodial sentence up to 10 years.

33 OJ L 376, 27 December 2006, p. 21.

34 OJ L 60, 28 February 2014, p. 34.

35 OJ L 133, 22 May 2008, p.66.

36 See also the case law from the European Court of Justice in this field of consumer credit, most recently the judgement in Case C-42/15, Home Credit Slovakia, a.s. v Klára Bíróová, and the judgement in Case C-377/14, Radlinger and Radlingerová v Finway a.s.

National legislation can establish other significant restrictions. Regarding prospecting and establishing business relationships, these obligations concern in particular the following areas:

- Advertising
- Cold calling. In most EU Member States, unsolicited calls are either subject to specific constraints or prohibited[37].
- Mass mailing. The possibility of sending mail or emails to a significant number of prospects can be severely restricted. In Austria, any dispatch to more than 50 recipients is problematic[38].
- Pre-contractual information. The relevant EU rules are often stricter when implemented at the national level.
- Language of contracts. In certain countries, clients may be required to sign contracts in their own language e.g. Spain.
- Content of contracts. Certain legal systems broaden the right of withdrawal. This is the case for German contract law[39].
- Formal validity of contracts. It might be that the regulation in certain countries imposes a particular form of contracts governing also financial services. Depending how the foreign bank is acting towards the target country, it might be that this formality applies to the agreement signed with the foreign service provider. For instance, Italian regulation foresees that some financial contracts have to be signed by the client and by the service provider.[40]
- Conditions for granting benefits. This concerns essentially national law on consumer credits, which may go beyond the EU directive.

Chapter 2: Applicability

Generally speaking, one can say that the rules on consumer protection covering the pre-contractual phase are absolute. UK firms prospecting clients in a Member State of the European Union must therefore comply with rules on advertising and on how to establish contact. The application of any other rules should be considered in the situations described in the preceding section on investor protection. Thus, a UK firm acting on the basis of a cross-border licence shall in most cases be required to comply with all national consumer protection rules[41].

---

37 For example in Austria: Par. 107(1) Telekommunikationsgesetz.

38 Par. 107(2)-(6) Telekommunikationsgesetz and par. 6 E-Commerce-Gesetz.

39 Art. 357 Bürgerliches Gesetzbuch.

40 See also art 11 of Regulation (EC) No 593/2008 of 17 June 2008 on the law applicable to contractual obligations (Rome I). See also in this context the recent rulings of the Italian Supreme Court Cass. civ. 24 March 2016, n. 5919, and Cass. civ. 27 April 2016, n. 8395.

41 For example in Luxembourg (Chap. II.4.b, Circ. CSSF 11/515).

Section E: Obstacles due to exchange control rules

Even if cross-border prospecting is permitted by financial regulations, it could be de facto severely restricted by local exchange control rules.

Exchange controls rules can have various purposes. They can either be exclusive, in the sense that they prohibit the opening of any account abroad or the transfer of any funds or any exchange transaction without prior approval of the central bank, or simply require notification, i.e. the person concerned is only obliged to notify the central bank of his country. These requirements entail multiple specific constraints in each country. Thus, the requirement to obtain authorisation only materialises when a certain annual amount is exceeded, which is the case in e.g. India[42] or Taiwan[43]. Obviously, the more stringent the exchange controls, the more they will have a practical negative effect on market access.

It is up to the client to comply with his country's foreign exchange rules. However, a clear violation of these restrictions can also constitute a risk factor for a foreign firm and thus limit its activity.

The EU does not have, as a political or monetary entity, any exchange controls. Article 63 FEU Treaty[44] guarantees the free movement of capital both within and outside the EU. Despite this, certain Member States have adopted very restrictive exchange control measures. This is the case for Greece[45] and Cyprus. In the latter country, restrictions were introduced in 2013 and lifted in 2015[46]. In the wider EEA, Iceland introduced restrictions in 2008 at the height of the financial crisis and lifted most of them in 2016[47] and 2017[48]. Other countries have introduced a notification system to the central bank of assets held on accounts opened abroad, e.g. Belgium[49] and Slovakia[50].

Foreign exchange control rules have nothing to do with the obligations under anti-money laundering regulation to disclose international transactions including cash movements. The

---

42 The Foreign Exchange Management Act of 1999 allows remittances on an annual basis with frequent adaptation of their volume (currently USD 200'000).

43 For Taiwan the annual amount is USD 5 million for a natural person and USD 50 million for a firm.

44 OJ C 236, 26 October 2012, p. 47.

45 Legislative Act regarding cash withdrawal and capital market restrictions dated 18 July 2015.

46 Decision of the Ministry of Finance of 6 April 2015.

47 Act No. 105/2016, amending the Foreign Exchange Act No. 87/1992; Central Bank of Iceland Rules No. 862/2016 on Foreign Exchange of 17 October 2016; Central Bank of Iceland Guidelines on the Foreign Exchange Act No. 87/1992, and Guidelines on Rules No. 862/2016 on Foreign Exchange, both published on 21 October 2016.

48 Technically, the Central Bank of Iceland issued on 12 March 2017 Rules No 200/2017 which grant exemptions to most of the capital controls specified in the Foreign Exchange Act No 87/1992.

49 Notification must be made at the central contact point of the BNB.

50 Foreign Exchange Act 202/1995.

aims are different: foreign exchange control rules aim at protecting the currency while AML rules aims to detect criminal assets and prevent terrorism and nowadays also tax evasion.[51]

Section F:
Obstacles due to anti-money laundering rules

Regulation for preventing the use of the financial system for the purposes of money laundering and terrorist financing is an indirect obstacle which materialises with increasing frequency. Its impact could legally limit a UK firm's operational capacity in a target country. In the context of Brexit in order to be judged as an equivalent jurisdiction as regards third-country equivalence, several EU legislative acts demand that the third-country AML framework is assessed. Therefore the UK's AML framework is likely to be assessed in the future. However, since the EU AML framework basically transposes the recommendations of the Financial Action Task Force (FATF) into EU law and future UK law is likely to also follow this global standard setter, EU-UK equivalence should be assumed in general.

In practice obtaining KYC and ID information[52] can be problematic. The increased level of due diligence required for foreign PEPs may pose particular difficulties.

In certain countries, AML regulations also apply to foreign institutions that take concrete steps with a view to establishing a business relationship. This mainly concerns situations where a UK firm has obtained a cross-border licence granted by local authorities. Such a firm could be obliged to report to local AML authorities based on the standards set in national laws and this could potentially conflict with confidentiality duties owed to a client.

This potential obstacle exists both in EU Member States and in other legal systems. In relation to banking, under English law, the contract between a bank and its customer is governed by

---

[51] The European Commission looks more closely at the question of national barriers to capital flows in the framework of the Capital Markets Union, see the respective report of 27 February 2017, COM(2017) 102. Also, the Economic and Financial Committee, an advisory body to the Council, examines on an annual basis the situation regarding the movement of capital and the freedom of payments, see the EFC Report of 14 March 2017, Ares(2017)1498797. As regards cash movements, on EU level there is Regulation (EC) No 1889/2005 of the European Parliament and of the Council of 26 October 2005 on controls of cash entering or leaving the Community (OJ L 309 of 25 November 2005, p. 9). For the main purpose of preventing money laundering, this Regulation requires natural persons entering or leaving the EU and carrying cash of a value of EUR 10,000 or more to declare that sum to the competent authorities.

[52] It may be worth noting that in the EU, since 2014 the eIDAS-Regulation (Regulation (EU) No 910/2014 of 23 July 2014 on electronic identification) sets standards for electronic identification and trust services for electronic transactions including electronic funds transfers. This Regulation does not harmonise customer authentication in the EU but aims at establishing interoperability between the different local systems. It is therefore only of secondary importance, however, after Brexit, to facilitate electronic funds transfers into the EU, UK firms should follow developments and the evolution of standards.

the laws of the place where the account is kept, in the absence of agreement to the contrary. The duty of a bank to keep its customer's affairs confidential is often merely an implied term of the contract between bank and customer. The duty is subject to an increasing number of exceptions, but otherwise extends to all information which the bank has about its customer. The exceptions include reporting duties in law dealing with anti-money laundering and the financing of terrorism. There is already some uncertainty in relation to UK AML law and its effect on customer relationships (see Shah vs HSBC Bank[53]) and cross-border activity makes the picture even more complex.

Note the situation in Luxembourg where the CSSF circular on the granting of a cross-border licence to non-EU countries also mentions, among the constraints that apply, compliance with Luxembourg AML rules[54]. The duty to report, pursuant directly or indirectly, to local AML law also exists in countries on other continents. South Africa, for example also requires foreign investment companies with a cross-border licence to comply with reporting duties according to local law[55].

Section G:
Obstacles due to data protection rules

The protection of personal data has been regulated in the EU since adoption in 1995 by means of the Data Protection Directive. The UK implemented this Directive via the Data Protection Act 1998. The EU recently changed its approach and replaced the Directive by a General Data Protection Regulation (GDPR)[56] and an accompanying Data Protection Directive in the area of law enforcement. The GDPR comes into force in the UK on 25 May 2018 and so will be implemented prior to the UK leaving the EU. The new framework continues to regulate the treatment of personal data of EU data subjects by EEA and non-EEA data controllers and processors, thus including data transfers to third countries. The rules apply when personal data is being processed in the context of the activities of a data controller and processor. This includes activities such as e-banking services and also the transfer of data for the purpose of facilitating cross-border banking or investment services.

Data transfers to third countries may take place provided that a number of conditions and safeguards are met. The European Commission must deliver adequacy decisions[57] and

53 Shah -v- HSBC Private Bank (UK) Limited [2012] EWHC 1283.

54 Chap. II.4.b, Circ. CSSF 11/515.

55 See: The Financial Intelligence Centre Act of 2001.

56 Due to the UK and Republic of Ireland's special status regarding justice and home affairs legislation, the Directive's provisions only apply in these countries to a limited extent. As for Iceland, Norway, Switzerland and Liechtenstein, the Directive constitutes a development of provisions of the Schengen aquis.

57 Currently the following countries qualify as adequate jurisdictions: Andorra, Argentina, Canada, Switzerland, Faroe Islands, Guernsey, Isle of Man, Israel, Jersey, New Zealand and Uruguay. As for the US, the "Privacy Shield" agreement between the EU and US replacing the "Safe Harbour"

approve model clauses for controller-to-controller/processor data transfers. At the time of Brexit, the UK would appear to be de facto equivalent by virtue of having implemented GDPR. However, a UK firm with no establishment in the EU will still have the obligation to appoint a representative in a Member State as the point of contact for the data protection authorities.

Third-country transfers are also possible if not frequent or material and, *inter alia*, consented to by the data subject and necessary to perform or enter into a contract with the data subject, or based on a code of conduct or certifications approved by the supervisory authority. A legal requirement from a third country is not a valid reason for a transfer unless it is based on an international agreement. Thus, even if a third country does not qualify as an adequate jurisdiction, the use of the official model clauses should facilitate data transfers.

After Brexit, the GDPR applies to UK financial intermediaries collecting data on EU clients for its own business thus having an extraterritorial impact. Note that the fine for a breach can be relevant (4 per cent of the firm's annual turnover). The establishment of a single data protection regime across the EU nonetheless has the advantage that only one set of rules has to be implemented by UK firms.

Section H:
Tax barriers

Finally, the cross-border activity of prospecting and establishing a relationship can, indirectly, be limited by obstacles due to tax regulations. This is not about the criminal risk incurred by a UK firm dealing with clients or prospects who are not tax compliant. It is a matter that is, strictly speaking, not related to market access. Nevertheless attention should be paid to the constraints or other factors that in reality impact the capacity to or interest in entering into a given market. One can distinguish three main obstacles:

Chapter 1: Permanent establishment

From a purely regulatory point of view, an intensive presence by employees of a foreign financial establishment in a client's country is possible, either because regulations permit it or because the bank has a cross-border licence that allows it. At a certain point, however, the tax authorities of the country may consider that this presence amounts to a permanent establishment. This would lead to local taxation of the revenues generated by such an activity. The tolerance threshold can be qualitative or quantitative. There are also specific provisions in double tax treaties. At the European level, there are most often qualitative

---

agreement was agreed in February 2016, but is not yet in effect. The European Commission published a draft "adequacy decision", declaring the agreement's provisions to be equivalent to the protections offered by EU law, but this is still open to challenge by European governments and data protection authorities.

thresholds, whereas in more exotic countries the presence thresholds are often more precise. In Indonesia, for example, a tax liability would exist when the representatives of the UK firm remain in Indonesia, in total and on a consolidated basis, for over 183 days per year[58]. It is often difficult to determine the tolerance threshold for countries without a numerical limit.

In any case, this obstacle does not prohibit any on-site prospecting activity, it only confronts the bank with a tax risk that must be taken into account.

Note however that some arrangements which appear to be tax efficient may have unforeseen consequences. When for example a UK bank makes a Lombard loan to an Italian taxpayer the passive interest is deductible for tax purposes by the borrower, but the bank is at risk of *de iure* a permanent establishment in Italy.

Chapter 2: Tax reporting and withholding of tax at source

An indirect limitation to establishing a relationship with foreign clients results from tax reporting requirements for an account or portfolio and any possible withholding taxes[59] that must be deducted, either according to local law, or simply to ensure an administrative service equivalent to that provided by banks in the client's country of residence. Promoting its services in a given country is only possible, *de facto*, if the bank is capable of assuming these tasks. This matter will not be developed any further in this paper.

Chapter 3: Double taxation agreements

Ideally, the situation of a taxpayer making investments from the UK should not greatly differ from that of a taxpayer in his country of residence. In fact, tax legislation – in particular in EU countries – tends to introduce differences in treatment, depending both on the origin of the income deriving from movable assets of their resident taxpayers and the location of the provider (the local or foreign bank) who pays over such revenue. Such differentiated systems obviously constitute barriers to prospecting and establishing a relationship with foreign clients. In particular, an obstacle to the promotion of the UK firm's services can result from the different treatment accorded to profits or losses on financial investments by the tax authorities in the client's country of residence, depending on the location of the account. If this disadvantage is significant, it will be very difficult for the bank to promote its services in this country[60].

---

58 Art. 2(3) Law No. 36 of 2008 on Income Tax Law.

59 Withholding taxes on cross-border securities income have been acknowledged by the European Commission as a trade barrier, however, prominently only in the area of post-trading. Due to the lack of competence in tax matters, no substantial developments have taken place at an EU level in this regard. See Commission Recommendation of 19.10.2009 on withholding tax relief procedures, C(2009)7924.

60 Uldry Serge, *Les limites de la conformité fiscal pour l'Espagne*, article published in Le Temps of 1 March 2013, p.14.

Chapter 4: Other tax barriers

Some EU countries could have an extraterritorial tax approach for specific taxation. For instance, Belgium has decided to make securities transactions undertaken for Belgian residents by foreign financial intermediaries subject to its tax on financial transactions (*Taxe sur les operations de bourse*, TOB[61]). Although the client is still the tax payer, this obligation can deter Belgian clients from investing abroad because of the administrative burden[62].

[61] Art. 120 et seq. of the Code des droits et taxes divers; Art. 128 et seq. of the Belgian programme law of 2016.

[62] Note that several EU Member States have introduced some kind of financial transaction tax which, however, differ in scope, tax base and tax rate and not necessarily have an extraterritorial impact. Efforts of all or some EU Member State to introduce a harmonised system of financial transaction tax have so far not been successful.

Part 4:
Duty to obtain a licence or registration in the EU

In this chapter we will return to consider in more detail one of the main regulatory obstacles that needs to be overcome to promote and establish business relationships in EU Member States. This concerns a firm's requirement to comply with financial services law and consequently to obtain a licence from the European supervisory authorities or those of the client's country of residence or where the client is physically situated. In order to do so, we will start by describing the EU legal regime regarding the provision of banking and investment services as well as the registration or notification requirements on financial instruments (Section A). We will then discuss national regulations (Section B).

Section A:
Licence or registration requirement as an EU constraint

A distinction must be made between the licence regime for banking services (Chapter 1) and for investment services (Chapter 2). Financial products meant for distribution usually must be registered or notified to the competent authority (Chapter 3). Under certain circumstances, it is sufficient that the authorisation or registration took place in the foreign country if the foreign country's jurisdiction has been recognised as equivalent by the EU (Chapter 4).

Chapter 1: EU licence regime for banking services

By banking services we primarily mean the taking of deposits from of the public (opening of accounts) with the aim of financing third parties with these deposits (credit activity). Maintaining an account also implies other ancillary services such as making payments, issuing cheques, granting guarantees etc. In the EU, these activities are governed primarily by the Capital Requirements Directive (CRD IV[63]). Other directives also regulate services that are part of the banking activities described above. We refer in particular to the Mortgage Credit Directive and the Consumer Credit Directive as well as the Payment Services Directive[64] and the Payment Accounts Directive[65]. The situation of a UK firm must be examined in light of

---

[63] Directive 2013/36/EU of the European Parliament and of the Council of 26 June 2013 on access to the activity of credit institutions and the prudential supervision of credit institutions and investment firms, OJ L 176, 27 June 2013, p. 338.

[64] Directive 2007/64/EC of the European Parliament and of the Council of 13 November 2007 on payment services in the internal market [PSD], OJ L 319, 5.12.2007, p. 1, and its successor as of 13 January 2018, Directive (EU) 2015/2366 of the European Parliament and of the Council of 25 November 2015 on payment services in the internal market [PSD II], OJ L 337, 23 December 2015, p. 35.

[65] Directive 2014/92/EU of the European Parliament and of the Council of 23 July 2014 on the comparability of fees related to payment accounts, payment account switching and access to payment accounts with basic features, OJ L 257, 28 August 2014, p. 214. The Payment Accounts

these texts. The purpose is essentially to understand which activities are subject to a licence in application of the EU texts.

1.1 CRD IV – Taking deposits and funds from the public

Credit institutions are primarily governed by the EU capital requirements regime (CRD IV and the Capital Requirements Regulation, CRR[66]) which transposes the Basel rules into EU law with certain add-ons. CRD IV is the basis for the requirement for a licence[67]. In order to understand the scope of this requirement with regard to a UK firm and the activities it intends to undertake, the following points must be considered:

- Pursuant to Article 8 CRD IV, *"Member States shall require credit institutions to obtain authorisation before commencing their activities."* The approach is simple and logical: within the territory of the Union it is prohibited to start an activity subject to a licence without having obtained prior authorisation. This provision obviously has an extraterritorial impact in that a non-European firm cannot commence activity as a credit institution in a Member State without obtaining authorisation from this Member State. This legal provision is however rather imprecise as to what constitutes commencement of banking activity, especially regarding the initial activity that we are interested in i.e. prospecting and establishing business relationships. The same applies to the concept of territorial link to a country: does the provision concern an activity performed on-site or on a remote basis? Finally, the provision seems to leave some discretion in relation to the concept of authorisation. Even though Articles 47 et seq., concerning the relationship with third countries, only mention authorisation in the form of a branch, no provision excludes authorisation in the form of a cross-border licence.
- Pursuant to Article 9 CRD IV, *"Member States shall prohibit persons or undertakings that are not credit institutions from carrying out the business of taking deposits or repayable funds from the public"*. This provision is the basis for the monopoly that banks have in relation to the receipt of funds from the public. Only authorised banks may undertake this activity. Conversely, other *banking* activities could as occur

Directive aims to improve the transparency and comparability of fee information about payment accounts, help customers switch payment accounts, and ensure every EU resident has access to a basic bank account. This directive has no authorisation element but affects certain aspects of offering payment services including the marketing thereof.

66 Regulation (EU) No 575/2013 of the European Parliament and of the Council of 26 June 2013 on prudential requirements for credit institutions and investment firms, OJ L 176, 27 June 2013, p. 1.

67 See Art. 4 and 14 of the SSM-Regulation (Council Regulation (EU) No 1024/2013 of 15 October 2013 conferring specific tasks on the European Central Bank concerning policies relating to the prudential supervision of credit institutions, OJ L 287, 29 October 2013, p. 63) for the role that the European Central Bank plays as regards the authorisation of banks in the Eurozone (Single Supervisory Mechanism). In a nutshell, the ECB authorises deposit taking credit institutions in cooperation with the national competent authority. The authorisation of other banking services remains sole competence of the national competent authority.

without a licence. It is up to each Member State to define which activities require a licence in addition to the activity of deposit taking.

- Annex 1 of CRD IV lists the activities that are subject to mutual recognition[68]. This list only has intra-European reach. The purpose is to allow credit institutions that intend to create a branch in other Member States, or benefit from the freedom to provide services, to provide an extensive range of services. It does not mean that Member States must grant authorisation for the activities listed, in addition to the activity of accepting deposits.

Once the UK has left the EU those UK banks with branches in EU countries set up using the passporting mechanism under CRD IV and its predecessors will have to assess their position. If such banks wish to maintain a permanent bank establishment in the relevant EU Member State they will have to either apply for recognition of the branch as a third country bank branch or subsidiarise the branch so that they have a full banking subsidiary in the country in question. It is possible that there may be special arrangements adopted as a consequence of the Brexit negotiations if the UK grants reciprocal access to EU banks, but this should not be assumed. If a UK bank only wants to engage in investment services rather than banking services there are mechanisms available for third-country access under MiFID II and MiFIR.

1.2 Other banking services

i. Mortgage loans

The purpose of the Mortgage Credit Directive is mainly to protect consumers borrowing in order to purchase real estate. At this point, however, the Directive is of interest to us because it introduces the principle of a licence or a registration for both non-credit institutions (Art. 35) and for credit intermediaries (Art. 29). This licence is necessary in order to operate in Member States.

The directive does not have any provisions concerning non-EU countries. However, it is easy to understand that it creates EU-wide restrictions in relation to residential mortgage loan activity. Even though the directive allows each Member State to transcribe it into national law, one can only assume that its reach towards third countries, in effect, goes further than CRD IV. If the debtor and the property are situated within the EU, there is an obvious link to the application of these provisions.

Without a licence, it is not possible for a UK firm to promote mortgage lending on residential property. Credit intermediaries cannot provide services to credit institutions that are not allowed to operate (Art. 32) within the EEA and, in addition, they must have their registered office in the country which registers them (Art. 29), which excludes any cross-border licence

68 These concern in particular: Lending, including consumer credit, credit agreements relating to immovable property, financial leasing, payment services, issuing other means of payment, guarantees, financial transactions on securities, participation in securities issues, advice to undertakings on capital structures, portfolio management and advice, safe custody service etc.

for this activity. In practice it seems clear that there has been little cross-border mortgage lending other than to the high net worth segment and so UK financial institutions may not need to concern themselves too much with this topic unless HNWI clients are a key constituent of their business model.

ii. Consumer credits

Directive 2008/48/EC concerns consumer protection in relation to consumer credit. This Directive applies to credit agreements with a consumer involving amounts EUR 200 or more but less than EUR 75'000 (Art. 2 (h)). The Directive introduced a pan-European regime for consumer lending and required some changes to the existing longstanding UK consumer credit regime. Article 20 of the Directive requires Member States to ensure that creditors are duly supervised. However, the provision does not exclude non-European creditors. It is thus up to each Member State to define its regulation on this point. The European Court of Justice has also established a considerable amount of case-law in this field, for example, on aspects such as pre-contractual information[69] or on foreign currency denominated loans[70]. In practice as is the situation for mortgage lending, cross-border consumer credit provision is not significant within the EU. Figures published by the European Commission in 2015 indicate that is constitutes less than 1 per cent of consumer lending. When the UK leaves the EU it seems unlikely that there would be a major increase in such lending by UK providers.

iii. Payment services

The Payment Services Directive (PSD II which applies as of 13 January 2018) grants consumers certain rights including the opening of a payment account with basic features with a credit institution or other type of payment services provider (Art. 1). PSD II only applies to non-EU banks or payment services providers which have a presence in the EU. There is no provision that, directly or indirectly, limits access to the European market for non-European service providers in relation to payment service activity, however, there is no third country passport available. The directive expands on the scope of its predecessor (Directive 2007/64/EC) and in particular introduces new concepts of interest to UK firms after Brexit: Banks with customer consent will be able to allow third-party access to accounts (third-party providers). By allowing access to accounts, PSD II enables payers to make payments using third-party payment initiation service providers and will also allow third parties to provide aggregated views of customer accounts. Furthermore, transactions in any currency where either the payer's or the recipient's payment service provider is located in the EU, irrespective of other providers located outside the EU, are within the scope of PSD II ('one-leg-out' or OLO payments). So UK banks and other UK payment services providers that will lose PSD

---

69 See also the case-law from the European Court of Justice in this field of consumer credit, most recently the judgement in Case C-42/15, Home Credit Slovakia, a.s. vs. Klára Bíróovà, and the judgement in Case C-377/14, Radlinger and Radlingerová v Finway a.s.

70 See the preliminary ruling in the case Banif Plus Bank Zrt. vs. Márton Lantos and Mártonné Lantos, Case C-312/14.

passporting rights after Brexit will therefore still be affected by EU payment services regulation.

The Interchange Fees Regulation[71] only regulates card-based payment transactions (debit and credit cards) where both the payer's and the payee's payment service provider are located within the EU. It introduces a cap on the interchange fees between these providers and UK payment service providers currently apply the requirements of this regulation. The regulation does not look at situations where one provider is located in a third country. However, it requires that the issuance of payment cards in third countries should be taken into account when assessing potential circumvention of the regulation (recital 31). After Brexit, this could de facto force UK payment service providers to continue applying caps on their transactions with EU counterparties.

As for the Single Euro Payments Area (SEPA)[72], the UK will lose its automatic qualification to be within the geographical scope of this area, but note that non-EU countries are currently within SEPA.

iv. Electronic money

In contrast to payment service providers, e-money institutions which are in the scope of the Second Electronic Money Directive[73] will lose all EU market access and must seek authorisation locally if possible.

1.3 Summary

EU regulations covering offers of banking services by a UK bank towards the EU can be summarised as follows:

- In relation to authorisation based on EU law, the activity of UK financial intermediaries would be limited by two principal restrictions: covering deposit taking and mortgage lending. With regard to these activities, post-Brexit a UK service provider would be obliged to obtain a licence – unless Brexit negotiations result in a cross-border license for UK banks resulting from an EU agreement with the UK to apply effectively the same treatment to UK banks as is given to EU banks. This agreement would imply UK equivalence with EU requirements and of course is not a forgone conclusion.

---

71 Regulation (EU) 2015/751 of the European Parliament and of the Council of 29 April 2015 on interchange fees for card-based payment transactions, OJ L 123 of 19 May 2015, p. 1.

72 Regulation (EU) No 260/2012 of the European Parliament and of the Council of 14 March 2012 establishing technical and business requirements for credit transfers and direct debits in euro, OJ L 94, 30 March 2012, p.22.

73 Directive 2009/110/EC of the European Parliament and of the Council of 16 September 2009 on the taking up, pursuit and prudential supervision of the business of electronic money institutions, OJ L 267 of 10 October 2009, p. 7.

- With regard to the promotion of other banking activities (non-mortgage credits etc.) licensing remains a national competence. There are also possible licensing issues relating to the cross-border provision of consumer credit and each EU country has its own approach to consumer credit provision by third-country institutions. In practice, there is little lending of this type.
- The question as to whether the activity of promoting banking services itself falls under the scope of authorisation requirements is a national competence. The same reasoning applies to the issue of territorial links with the EU.

Chapter 2: EU licence regime for investment services

Investment services include amongst other activities: reception and transmission of orders in financial instruments, execution of orders, investment advice and discretionary asset management. At EU level, the future promotion of these services by a non-EU service provider must be examined with regard to two pieces of EU legislation: the Markets in Financial Instruments Regulation (hereafter: MiFIR)[74] and the Markets in Financial Instruments Directive (hereafter: MiFID II)[75].

2.1 MiFIR

This regulation includes within its scope the provision of investment services by third-country firms to eligible counterparties and per se professional investors established in the EU (Art. 1(1) (f)). The concept of investment services is defined by reference to MiFID II (Art. 2). The provision of services to other categories of investors (retail clients and elective professional clients) is covered by MiFID II.

MiFIR has a two pronged approach to access to the European market by non-EU service providers:

- the first approach originates from EU law. Pursuant to Article 46(1), "*A third-country firm may provide investment services or perform investment activities with or without any ancillary services to eligible counterparties and to professional clients within the meaning of Section I of Annex II to Directive 2014/65/EU established throughout the Union without the establishment of a branch where it is registered in the register of third-country firms kept by ESMA in accordance with Article 47.*" So provided it is registered with ESMA, a post-Brexit UK firm may engage with its target clientele within any EU member state. MIFIR grants a passport without any physical presence; a cross-border licence valid for the whole European territory. Registration with ESMA is however subject to the essential condition that the UK obtains an equivalence

74 Regulation (EU) No 600/2014 of the European Parliament and of the Council of 15 May 2014 on markets in financial instruments, OJ L 173, 12 June 2014, p. 84.

75 Directive 2014/65/EU of the European Parliament and of the Council of 15 May 2014 on markets in financial instruments, OJ L 173, 12 June 2014, p. 349.

decision from the European Commission (Art. 47). A summary of the requirements of the MiFIR third-country passport is provided in the following table.

- the second approach is a national one. If there is no registration with ESMA, in particular due to the absence of an equivalence decision, Member States may authorise third-country firms to "provide" or to "perform" investment services, together with ancillary services, to eligible counterparties and elective professional clients on the Member State's national territory (Art. 46(4)). This is nationally based authorisation without any pan-European dimension. We note that under MiFIR Member States cannot permit any offering or servicing activity without authorisation. Prospecting clearly becomes an activity subject to authorisation. The term "in its territory" used by MiFIR nevertheless leaves scope for appreciation as to the point at which a territorial link triggers the need for authorisation. Prospecting via remote means of communication could, according to varying national interpretations, also be exempt from authorisation. MiFIR provides full flexibility regarding the conditions for and the scope of such an authorisation. We also note that this is simply a protestative condition and that an EU country may decide to simply prohibit any prospecting activity from overseas.
- common approach. Parallel to MiFID II, the MiFIR contains a general exemption for reverse solicitation which will be described hereafter.

Finally, it must be emphasised that MiFIR, as an EU regulation, is directly applicable in all EU Member States, with no need for transposition into national law.

Table: MiFIR third country services passport for investment services to eligible counterparties and per se professional clients (Art. 46 and 47 MiFIR)

Steps	Content
Equivalence assessment by ESAs	Mandated by the European Commission. There is no mandatory timeframe and so an assessment could take a number of months or even years. ESMA is likely to conduct MiFID II and MiFIR assessments and the EBA CRD assessments.
Equivalence decision by COM	(1) Review legal and supervisory arrangements of the third country, third country firms must comply with legally binding prudential and business conduct requirements: – Comparison of framework with MiFID II, MiFIR and CRD; – "Prudential and business conduct framework": • Authorisation, supervision, enforcement on ongoing basis • Sufficient capital requirements, appropriate requirements on shareholders and management body • Adequate organisational requirements in the area of internal control functions • Appropriate conduct of business rules • Preventing market abuse
	(2) Cooperation arrangements between ESMA and third country competent authority: – Access to all information, mechanism for info exchange – Mechanism for prompt notification in case of infringements – Coordination of supervisory activities including onsite inspections
	(3) Arrangements for withdrawal of decision.
Registration with ESMA	– Application as for an EU passport – No additional requirements imposed by Member States, but no favourable treatment in comparison with EU firm – Completeness of application confirmed within 30 business days, registration granted or refused within 180 business days – Firms must inform clients about limited passport – Firms must offer clients jurisdiction of court or arbitral tribunal in a Member State
Withdrawal of registration	– Documented evidence that firm is prejudicing investor interests or the functioning of orderly markets – Serious infringement of applicable provisions – Third-country competent authority has not taken action or has not delivered a counterproof – Third-country competent authority must be informed 30 days before withdrawal – COM must review third-country equivalence afterwards

2.2 MiFID II

Regarding access to the European market from third countries after 2018, the revised MiFID will apply when post-Brexit UK firms prospect retail clients, including those who could opt-up to professional status (under MiFID Annex 2 section II). The MiFID II authorisation regime is based on the following principles:

- ***Restrictions on unauthorised investment services***. According to Article 5(1) MiFID II *"each Member State shall require that the provision of investment services and/or the performance of investment activities as a regular occupation or business on a professional basis be subject to prior authorisation"*. The authorisation is valid in the territory of the Union and allows an authorised firm to provide the investment services listed in the licence through a branch or *"through the freedom to provide services"*. The provision is however imprecise with regard to the frequency and professional nature of any activities performed and also with regard to what type of geographical link with the EU could trigger a requirement. The authorisation requirement only covers those investment services listed in section A of Annex 1 of the directive and defined in Article 4 of the directive. The definition of "investment advice" merits special attention. The Directive defines it as *"the provision of personal recommendations to a client, either upon its request or at the initiative of the investment firm, in respect of one or more transactions relating to financial instruments"*. This means that the provision of non-personal recommendations is not subject to MiFID II restrictions. Any type of general recommendation constitutes an ancillary service only.[76] EU Member States remain entirely to decide whether to regulate the cross-border offer and provision of these services.
- *Ancillary services and other services.* EU level restrictions do not cover ancillary services and other services. An offer of ancillary services by a non-EU firm is only subject to a licence on the basis of national law. Amongst ancillary services, it is worth mentioning the maintenance of securities accounts. It is clear that this is subject to neither CRD IV, nor MiFID II authorisation.
- *Limits to EU level authorisation requirements - national assessment.* Currently, Member States enjoy a certain margin of discretion as to the point from which an investment activity directed towards a given country requires a licence. Under MiFID II this is explicit as Article 39 specifies that each Member State *"may"* require that third-country firms that provide investment services or perform investment activities with or without any ancillary services "in its territory" establish a branch. It is open to EU countries whether to exercise this option and

[76] The definition of an « investment recommendation » is a term originating in the EU market abuse framework, currently regulated in Regulation (EU) No 596/2014 (Market Abuse Regulation, MAR). See Art. 3(1)(35) MAR. When disseminating investment recommendations into the EU – including to the public –, a firm therefore always has to keep in mind that it is not based on inside information in the sense of this Regulation and that it is objectively presented, i.e. disclosing any conflict of interest.

indeed some countries may choose to have other types of licence requirements where there is no physical presence in the country in question. Even though the geographical link between a firm's activity and the target country is also subject to interpretation, it should be pointed out that the initial activity of prospecting is clearly covered as Article 39 covers thirds country firms "**intending** to provide investment services or perform investment activities with or without any ancillary services". In any case, Member States have freedom, for the time being, to decide on their authorisation policy regarding the prospecting activity of non-EU firms.

- *Exemption for reverse solicitation*. According to Article 42 MiFID II, the provision of an investment service or activity by a non-EU firm "*at the exclusive initiative of the client*" is not subject to authorisation. The terms used suggest the recognition of an absolute right to serve the client upon his request. Pending official interpretation, we are convinced that this provision cannot permit a third-country firm to propose its services in the territory of a Member State without any restrictions. Again, each Member State has broad discretion regarding the implementation of this provision. This freedom of interpretation also affects another aspect of Article 42 (i.e. restrictions regarding the scope of reverse solicitation) which specifies that "*an initiative by such clients shall not entitle the third-country firm to market otherwise than through the branch, where one is required in accordance with national law, new categories of investment products or investment services to that client*." So the exclusive initiative test applies on a service/activity basis - multiple services cannot be provided as a result of reverse solicitation relating to one particular service. It is not therefore a business model, but should be used on an exceptional basis.
- *MiFID II and MIFIR implementation in the UK*. As the UK is still a member of the EU it is implementing the MiFID II package in full. MiFIR and most of the accompanying Level 2 delegated acts apply directly in the EU Member States while MiFID II has to be implemented at the national level. The UK is doing or has done this by changing the primary relevant law – the Financial Services and Markets Act 2000 – and related secondary legislation such as the Regulated Activities Order. The FCA is also making numerous changes to various modules of its Handbook and the Prudential Regulatory Authority will implement certain changes to prudential rules where it has responsibility for systemically important investment firms. It is noteworthy that the UK, in line with its past practice, is extending the scope of some MiFID II requirements beyond what is required by the directive itself. Just to give two examples out of many, the UK telephone recording requirements will cover a wider range of activities and staff than required at the EU level and will apply to UK only investment advisers that are not subject to MiFID. Best execution standards will also apply to non-MiFID business. The FCA is at the time of writing still consulting on MiFID II implementation. It seems reasonable to assume full implementation of MiFID II in the UK with the proviso that UK firms will not be able to make use of cross-border mechanisms such as passporting.

2.3 Summary

EU regulation regarding offers of investment services by a post-Brexit UK firm can be summarised as follows:

- The activity of such firms is governed solely by EU law if the firm deals only with eligible clients and per se professionals, on the basis of authorisation by ESMA.
- In all other cases, the promotion of investment services could breach EU level restrictions, depending on the interpretation at national level.
- True and genuine reverse solicitation is a recognised safe harbour towards all clients.
- For those financial services that are not investment services within the meaning of MiFID II, Member States have full legislative freedom. Third-country service providers will therefore have to assess and take into account the situation in each target country.

Table: Market access for third-country firms under MiFID II and MiFIR

Reverse solicitation:	Per se professional investors and eligible counterparties:	Opt-up professional and retail investors:
– No local registration required when acting within the concept of reverse solicitation as understood in the target country – Member State may differ in interpreting this concept	– Equivalence assessment by ESMA and equivalence decision by COM – Transitional period for 3 years after equivalence decision – Finally: EU competence, registration with ESMA, certain conditions apply, third-country passport	– No equivalence decision – Member State competence – Member State may implement a branch requirement – No third-country passport
Art. 46 MiFIR, 42 MiFID II	Art. 46 et seq. MiFIR	Art. 39 et seq. MiFID II

Chapter 3: EU registration and notification requirements for financial products

Financial products are subject to EU level regulation and notably the UCITS Directive in its various iterations has been a great success leading to widespread brand recognition and cross-border sales.

The main areas of interest are:

3.1 Prospectuses

In the EU, the marketing of *transferable securities* must comply with the requirements of the Prospectus Directive[77]. Transferable securities may only be offered to the public or admitted to trading on a regulated market in the EU and EU-wide[78] if a prospectus is drawn up and notified to the competent authority. The purpose of the Prospectus Directive was to ease capital raising across the EU by introducing a "passport" for prospectuses. It provides cost-effective capital raising for issuers and enhances investor protection by requiring harmonised high standards of disclosure for issues of securities that are offered to the EU public or admitted to trading on an EU regulated market.

Third-country issuers may get approval for their prospectuses provided that certain conditions are fulfilled such as that the information requirements are equivalent to those in the EU. The Capital Markets Union (CMU) project aims to introduce further simplification of the current regime. UK issuers should be able to use this route, but it will be more expensive than the current option under which a "passported" prospectus is valid for the public offer or the admission of securities to trading in another Member State, provided the competent authority in the host Member State is notified.

The Prospectus Directive sets out a rather narrow range of exemptions for private placements. There are various exemptions from the requirement to produce a prospectus (e.g. the offer is made to qualified investors; the offer is made to fewer than 150 natural or legal persons other than qualified investors; the offer is made to investors who acquire the securities for a total consideration of at least EUR1000,000 etc.). The Prospectus Directive will be replaced by the Prospectus Regulation which will apply from a date in 2019 to be determined. The EUR100,000 minimum denomination safe harbour from the prospectus requirement will be retained as will the other exemptions mentioned above.

3.2 Alternative investment funds

Investment funds in the EU must be either a UCITS or an AIF which means that they are regulated either by the UCITS Directive or the AIFM Directive and the respective local transposition. The Alternative Investment Funds Managers Directive (AIFMD) has harmonised the regulation of alternative investment fund managers who manage or distribute alternative investment funds in the EU and affects non-EU as well as EU AIFMs and AIFs. For marketing an AIF, the AIFMD passport is currently only available to EU AIFMs when marketing EU AIFs to professional investors although certain countries allow marketing to other investor types, e.g.

---

[77] Directive 2003/71/EC of the European Parliament and of the Council of 4 November 2003 on the prospectus to be published when securities are offered to the public or admitted to trading, OJ L 345, 31 December 2003, p. 64.

[78] Articles 17 et seq. Prospectus Directive.

to semi-professional investors in Germany or to retail investors in the UK (subject to conditions).

Currently a non-EU AIFM may only market a non-EU AIF to EU professional investors under Member States' private placement regimes subject to various conditions: e.g. compliance with disclosure and reporting requirements; requirements on portfolio company disclosure and asset stripping; existence of a co-operation agreement between the relevant regulators, etc. The non-EU AIFM and, where relevant, the non-EU AIF must not be established in a country designated as non-cooperative by FATF. In addition, Member States may impose further stricter marketing requirements on a non-EU AIFM.

AIFMD has a mechanism for recognition of passporting for third country AIFMs in EU equivalent jurisdictions. Each jurisdiction is subject to an equivalence assessment. In July 2016, the European Securities and Markets Authority (ESMA) issued a recommendation relating to 12 third countries following up an earlier recommendation on the extension of the EU passport covering 6 third countries. The European Commission has the responsibility to enact a delegated act within three months according to AIFMD to formalise recognition of third countries.
However, as yet there has been no delegated act and it is unclear when one may appear.

Overall when the UK becomes a third country it would be reasonable to expect equivalence under AIFMD to be granted readily for after all the UK has fully implemented this Directive during its EU membership. However as the equivalence process is subject to bureaucratic and political hurdles nothing can be assumed.

3.3 Undertakings for Collective Investments in Transferable Securities

Under the UCITS Directive there is no third-country passport for UCITS compliant funds. A fund has to be established in the EEA to benefit from this passport. After Brexit UK UCITS funds will become non-EEA AIFs and so will only be able to passport under the AIFMD third-country regime.

Following Brexit, UK UCITS will become non-EU AIFs and may profit from the AIFMD third-country passport. In the absence of third-country passporting, national private placement regimes may provide a safe harbour. However, the AIFMD requires Member States to remove this option in due course and some countries such as Germany have already done so. Delegation of portfolio management services to third-country firms under certain conditions is possible under existing legislation, albeit subject to possible future unilateral changes by the EU legislators. It should be noted, however, that fund marketing is often via a MiFID investment firm and since marketing is not an investment service passported under MiFID, such activity is dependent on whether local law accepts marketing.

3.4 Other products

EU law also recognises specialist fund types which are not available for use by non-EU CIS. The EuVECA[79] and EuSEF[80] Regulations (European Venture Capital Funds and European Social Entrepreneurship Funds) contain requirements applying to the manager of qualifying funds who want to use such a designation covering the marketing of such funds, as well as registration of the manager.[81] The fund must be established on the territory of the EU and the manager must register with the competent authority of an EU Member State. Third-country managers cannot market a fund with such a designation on a cross-border basis in the EU and there is also no special registration for third-country managers with ESMA. Under the ELTIF[82] label (European Long-term Investment Funds), qualifying funds can be marketed in the EU using this designation only when they are authorised as such and only EU AIFs can be authorised as ELTIFs. Only an EU AIFM can apply for approval to manage an ELTIF.[83] Under the MMF Regulation[84], EU money market funds are structured as either UCITS or AIFs and must be authorised as such under the appropriate directive and then must fulfil further conditions under the MMF Regulation[85]. For the sake of brevity, we will not deal with these in further detail in this paper and would only mention that as yet these types of fund are relatively rare and not available for cross-border marketing by non-EU managers.

Finally, there is a proposed EU regulation creating a label for safe, transparent and standardised (STS) securitisations that is still at the proposal phase[86]. This proposal provides essentially for a system that is open to third-country securitisations. EU institutional investors can invest in non-EU securitisations and will have to perform the same due diligence as for EU securitisations, including a check whether the risk is retained and whether the originator, sponsor and special purpose entity make available all relevant information. Moreover, non-EU securitisations can also meet the STS requirements and the originator, sponsor and special purpose entity may also submit an STS notification to ESMA. There is also no requirement that the underlying exposures are located in the EU.

---

79 Regulation (EU) No 345/2013 of the European Parliament and of the Council of 17 April 2013 on European venture capital funds, OJ L 115, 25 April 2013, p. 1.

80 Regulation (EU) No 346/2013 of the European Parliament and of the Council of 17 April 2013 on European social entrepreneurship funds, OJ L 115, 25 April 2013, p. 18.

81 Article 14 EuVECA-Regulation, Article 15 EuSEF-Regulation

82 Regulation (EU) 2015/760 of the European Parliament and of the Council of 29 April 2015 on European long-term investment funds, OJ L 123, 19 May 2015, p. 98.

83 Articles 3-7 ELTIF-Regulation

84 Proposal for a Regulation of the European Parliament and of the Council on Money Market Funds, COM/2013/0615. The co-legislators agreed on the final version of this regulation in April 2017.

85 Articles 3 et seq. MMF-Regulation

86 Proposal for a Regulation of the European Parliament and of the Council laying down common rules on securitisation and creating a European framework for simple, transparent and standardised securitisation, COM(2015) 472.

3.5 Product intervention on EU level

Although they do not constitute product approval or licensing, it is important to note that, alongside national competent authorities, the European supervisory authorities (ESAs) were given market and product intervention powers under MiFIR[87], the PRIIPs Regulation[88] and the Short Selling Regulation[89]. This includes the task of monitoring financial markets in the EU as a whole. In addition, there are powers to temporarily prohibit or restrict the marketing, sale or sale of certain financial instruments, structured deposits or insurance products under pre-determined conditions in the event of significant concerns with regard to investor protection or a threat to the proper functioning or integrity of the financial and commodity markets or the stability of the whole financial system in the EU or part thereof. These powers do not only relate to products, but also to related activities. The ESAs' powers under MiFIR do not apply until 3 January 2018, however, those under PRIIPs apply as of 31 December 2016. ESA powers of intervention are subsidiary to actions taken by national competent authorities and are of an exceptional and precautionary nature. ESA intervention is only permitted if existing regulatory requirements do not address the threat and the national supervisory authorities have remained idle. The ESA must first notify the national supervisory authorities and publish its intervention on its website. It must check the operation of the intervention at least every three months. Lawful intervention by an ESA may precede action by national supervisory authorities.

In this context, it is worth noting that in practice, ESMA has so far issued statements and warnings on CfDs, binary options[90], contingent convertible instruments[91] and securities subject to the EU bank resolution framework[92], usually as far as their sale to consumers is concerned. Virtual currencies have been subject to an EBA warning[93].

---

87 See Art. 39-43 MiFIR; Art. 19-21 of Commission Delegated Regulation (EC) No ... / ... of 18.5.2016 supplementing [MiFIR] with regard to definitions, transparency, portfolio compression and supervisory measures on product intervention and positions, C(2016) 2860; ESMA Opinion Impact of the exclusion of fund management companies from the scope of the MiFIR Intervention Powers, ESMA50-1215332076-23.

88 See Art. 16(8), 17(7) of Regulation (EU) No 1286/2014 of the European Parliament and of the Council on key information documents for packaged retail and insurance-based investment products (PRIIPs); Commission Delegated Regulation (EU) 2016/1904 of 14 July 2016 supplementing Regulation (EU) No 1286/2014 of the European Parliament and of the Council with regard to product intervention.

89 See Art. 27-31 Short Selling Regulation and ECJ judgment C-270/12.

90 Warning about CfDs, binary options and other speculative products, ESMA/2016/1166 and ESMA/2016/1167 ; see also ESMA Questions and Answers Relating to the provision of CfDs and other speculative products to retail investors under MiFID (latest version of 31 March 2017, ESMA35-36-794) and the ESMA investor warning of 7 February 2014 on risks of investing in complex products.

91 Potential Risks Associated with Investing in Contingent Convertible Instruments, ESMA/2014/944.

92 MiFID practices for firms selling financial instruments subject to the BRRD resolution regime, ESMA/2016/902 and ESMA/2016/903.

93 Warning to consumers on virtual currencies, EBA/WRG/2013/01.

3.6 Additional aspects

Legislative acts such as the Benchmarks Regulation[94] or the Regulation on Credit Rating Agencies[95] do not constitute product approval or licensing, but have an effect on product sales into the EU. In order for a benchmark provided by an administrator located in a third country to be used within the EU – such as LIBOR after Brexit – the benchmark and the administrator must be registered with ESMA and hence fulfil certain conditions. The use of a benchmark such as LIBOR thus depends on the equivalence of the UK regulatory framework in this regard. This does not seem to cause too many headaches at the moment, however, UK firms wishing to sell products into the EU referring to such a benchmark are thus indirectly depending on relevant EU regulation. The situation is similar for credit ratings where third-country credit ratings agencies must be certified with ESMA or where a rating agency located in the EU may endorse[96] credit ratings issued in a third country only if certain conditions are fulfilled such as the equivalence of the relevant jurisdiction.
Although the PRIPs Regulation does not cover product authorisation it does affect the manufacturing and distribution of products by requiring the provision of a key investor information document (KID) to retail investors. After Brexit, this Regulation is not directly applicable to product manufacturers in the UK, however, there will be touchpoints e.g. when a UK product manufacturer collaborates with an EU distributor and must provide this distributor with the necessary information, or where a UK investment firm actively promotes products towards EU clients, where allowed.

Chapter 4: Equivalence

4.1 Concept of equivalence

The concept of equivalence does not grant comparable rights to passporting. Equivalence can only be requested by third countries where it is explicitly provided for in EU legislation. Equivalence provisions are tailored to the needs of each specific act and their meaning varies from one legal text to another. In contrast to passporting, equivalence does not cover all services or all client types and in general doesn't explicitly apply to retail financial services activities. Equivalence is often conditional on reciprocity by the third country. It is assessed by the European Commission based on advice by the relevant European Supervisory Authority and can theoretically be withdrawn at any time[97].

---

94 Regulation (EU) 2016/1011 of the European Parliament and of the Council of 8 June 2016 on indices used as benchmarks in financial instruments and financial contracts or to measure the performance of investment funds

95 Regulation (EC) No 1060/2009 of the European Parliament and of the Council of 16 September 2009 on credit rating agencies.

96 See ESMA Guidelines on the application of the endorsement regime under Article 4(3) of the Credit Rating Agencies Regulation No 1060/2009, ESMA/2011/139.

97 European Parliament Briefing Third-country equivalence in EU banking legislation, March 2017, PE 587.369

Considerations of what equivalence is and how it is applied and interpreted are important when analysing access by third country entities to the EU market, in particular for marketing of services and products:

> Under MIFID II/MIFIR in order to utilise the cross-border passport available to third-country firms for marketing to per se professional and eligible counterparties a positive equivalence determination by ESMA that the legal and supervisory arrangements in the third country have equivalent effect to MIFID II/MiFIR is needed.
> Under the AIFMD a country-by–country assessment is needed to enable use of the third country marketing passport.
> CRD IV/CRR equivalence clauses focus on the prudential treatment of certain types of exposures to entities located in third countries and are irrelevant as regards EU market access for third country firms.

There are various other EU level legislative acts[98] which touch on equivalence such as the European Markets Infrastructure Regulation (EMIR) and the above mentioned EU Benchmarks Regulation in force from 2018. However, in most cases assessing the equivalence of third-country regulatory frameworks primarily serve prudential regulatory purposes and do not grant market access to financial services providers. The following table gives an overview of relevant EU legislation and any equivalence mechanism for granting market access to third-country firms.

Table: Equivalence clauses in EU financial legislation relevant for market access

EU legislation	Equivalence clauses	Market access
Investment services		
MiFID II	–	Providing services to retail clients and opt up professional clients: subject to local law
MiFIR	+	Providing services to per se professional clients and eligible counterparties: third-country passport or, if passport is not available, subject to local law
Banking services		
CRD IV/CRR	+ but not for providing services	Subject to local law
CCD	–	Subject to local law

98 For an overview see the Commission Staff Working Document, EU equivalence decisions in financial services policy: an assessment, SWD(2017) 102, or European Parliament Briefing, Third-country equivalence in EU banking legislation, March 2017, PE 587.369. See also Understanding equivalence and the single passport in financial services, third-country access to the single market, European Parliamentary Research Service, February 2017; The UK's potential withdrawal from the EU and Single Market Access under EU financial services legislation, January 2017; Potential concepts for the future EU-UK relationship in financial services, January 2017.

MCD	–	Subject to local law
Payment services		
PSD II	–	Transactions in the currency of an EEA Member State may be treated as 'one-leg-out' (OLO) payments and PSD II partially applies
EMD II	–	Subject to local law
Asset management		
AIFMD	+	Possibility of extending the passport to non-EU fund managers otherwise subject to national private placement regimes
UCITS	–	–
Markets infrastructure		
EMIR	+	Passport-like rights for CCPs
Insurance services		
Solvency II	+	Reinsurers from third countries can be recognised as equivalent
IDD	–	Subject to local law

4.2 Assessment procedure[99]

The European Commission is responsible for carrying out technical assessments of equivalence. Such assessments are usually based on advice from one of the European Supervisory Authorities. Equivalence provisions typically require an assessment whether the requirements of a third-country framework are legally binding, subject to effective supervision by local authorities and achieve the same results as the EU rules in question. They set the criteria for the assessment and also confer to the European Commission discretion whether to grant equivalence or not. The decision may specify whether equivalence is granted in full or partially, for an indefinite period or with a time limit. The timeline required to obtain an equivalence decision varies and the Commission is not obliged to decide by a specific deadline.[100] The Commission also has the power to withdraw an equivalence decision often on a short time scale. Under some legislative acts, individual firms have to register with ESMA following an equivalence decision. The application for registration can require the fulfilment of further conditions as for the MiFIR third-country passport where firms will be required to, inter alia, offer clients jurisdiction of a court or arbitration tribunal in an EU Member State.

99 European Parliament Briefing, Third-country equivalence in EU banking legislation, March 2017, PE 587.369.

100 Until February 2017, the European Commission had adopted 212 equivalence decisions covering a total of 32 countries. Japan, US and Canada are the countries with the highest number of equivalence decisions. See European Parliament Briefing, Third-country equivalence in EU banking legislation, March 2017, PE 587.369.

4.3 Conclusion

It seems clear that there are practical issues with regard to equivalence determinations including the variation in the understanding of equivalence between various EU level requirements, the complexity and delays inherent in the process for recognising equivalence, the influence of subjective considerations such as EU and domestic politics on equivalence determinations and the lack of recognition of the benefits of mutual acceptance of equivalence.

The UK will be in an unusual position after Brexit as its regulatory regime will *prima facie* meet the same standards as that in the EU, so there is an opportunity for all parties involved to build a pragmatic and flexible equivalence model to reflect this. The concept of equivalence as it stands would, however, make the UK a rule-taker which might not be an acceptable basis for the UK's future relationship with the EU. Likewise, certain conditions attached to market access based on equivalence decisions such as having an arbitration tribunal in an EU Member State seem unattractive for UK firms. Furthermore, depending on equivalence assessments by foreign regulators and the inherent risk of changes to equivalence determinations does not appear to be a long-term or stable business model for UK financial intermediaries. In this sense, the UK trade minister *Mark Garnier* is quoted saying that equivalence is not going to be "good enough" for banks and suggested a "hybrid version" that would be designed especially for banks based in the UK.[101]

As neither the industry nor UK and EU authorities are content with current equivalence arrangements these are likely to change and due to the size of the UK's financial services sector it is likely to be treated as a special case. Certain EU sources and national regulators have indicated that the various third-country arrangements are not designed to accommodate a country such as the UK which has the largest financial services sector of any current EU member becoming a third country[102]. Negotiations are likely to take account of issues such as the need for ongoing EU/UK regulatory cooperation including supervision arrangements and data exchange, the likelihood that the UK will not be a passive rule taker, the need to depoliticise equivalence including an increased role for IOSCO and similar global bodies as standard setters, and the desire to maintain frictionless markets as far as is possible.

---

101 Mark Garnier said: "If we can create a special hybrid version of that, with a better version of equivalence or a different version of passporting, then that's what we will try to achieve. What we are not trying to do is fit into an existing box. We are trying to create a new model.", European Parliament Briefing, Third-country equivalence in EU banking legislation, March 2017, PE 587.369; Bloomberg, Banks Likely to Lose Passporting With Brexit, Official Says, 26 October 2016 (accessed on www.bloomberg.com on 24 March 2017).

102 Statement by Gérard Rameix Chairman of the AMF 24/03/2017 at Chatham House.

Section B:
Licence or registration requirements at the national level

We have just seen that EU law, whilst setting out the basis requirements to obtain a licence in order to operate in the EU from a third-country, does allow Member States a certain amount of discretion to define the limits of this obligation for the services that are subject to EU level restrictions. UK firms that intend to prospect the European market in order to establish a business relationship in the EU must therefore understand the national law of each target country. We have also seen that foreign products might need to be registered in application of EU and national law.

The purpose of this section is to provide a brief outline regarding the various approaches adopted. First of all, it is necessary to understand the regulatory approach with regard to the various services that may be offered (Chapter 1) and products that may be distributed (Chapter 2). Furthermore, it is in a firm's interest to understand from which point on it requires a licence and whether any safe harbours exist (Chapter 3). If authorisation is required, the UK service provider must enquire if it is possible to obtain a cross-border licence without a local corporate presence.

Before dealing with these issues, we wish to underline that at the time of writing, certain directives described above have not yet been transposed into national law. Our analysis will thus have to be updated after completion of this transposition. We have included some discussion on equivalence as it is a key consideration for third country financial services entities.

Chapter 1: Services subject to licensing

In order to comply with EU law, Member States must request a licence for services that are regulated by European legislative instruments. In all other cases, they are free to define which activities require a financial services licence.

1.1 Banking services

The EU level restrictions in the relevant directives are limited to deposit acceptance. National legislatures and regulators therefore have full discretion to decide what other credit activities require a licence by including them, for example, in the legal concept of a "bank". Credit activity without any collection of funds can thus be exempt from the authorisation regime which, in turn, implies that the foreign service provider can offer the credit in question freely. However, the tendency in Member States is to extend the obligation to obtain a licence to credit activities. In Germany, the cross-border activity of a Swiss credit provider was subject to an important court ruling recognising the validity of BaFin's decision on licensing[103]. Even where both credit activity and deposit taking from the public are subject to national law,

[103] Decision of the Bundesverwaltungsgericht of 22 April 2009 in re Fidium Finanz (BVerwG 8 C 2.09)

there can be differences regarding licensing requirements for cross-border activity directed towards such a country. An example is Hungary, which has a very restrictive approach regarding the provision of cross-border banking services, with the exception of certain credit activities. A third-country service provider can freely promote and grant credits in Hungary, provided that he is subject to supervision in his country of incorporation and that he informs the Hungarian regulator of this activity[104].

1.2 Investment services

In relation to investment services although these are defined at the EU level in MiFID II there are major discrepancies at the national level regarding the practical application of these definitions and the interpretation thereof. For example, as already discussed above, there is debate over the provision of a "*personal recommendation*" (art. 4(4) MiFID II), remember that a general recommendation is only an ancillary activity according to section B of annex 1 of MiFID II and thus doesn't require a licence. In Italy, the legislator specifies that there is a personal recommendation, and thus a licensing requirement, if the recommendation takes account of the client's situation. On the contrary, it is not personal if it is, as such, publicly disseminated[105]. The concept is very broad and, as a result, provision of financial information on financial instruments, including distribution of research material, could rapidly lead to the provision of a regulated service if it is addressed to a specific client. A similar situation exists in Austria[106]. Other Member States such as the Czech Republic, on the other hand, clearly consider the handing out of research or other generic material as a non-regulated activity[107].

1.3 Other services

Member States are also free to legislate in areas that are not covered by EU financial services law.

In Belgium, wealth planning has been subject to authorisation since 2014[108]. According to the Belgian legislator, "*a financial planning consultation is a consultation on the optimisation, in particular of the structuring, planning over time, protection, legal organisation or transmission of client's assets, according to the needs and objectives expressed by the client, excluding any provision of investment services or advice on transactions or on individual financial products*".[109] Even if the regulator considers that this activity is included in the list of activities

---

104 Chap. 4.3, Loi CCXXVII de 2013 sur les établissements de crédit et les entreprises financières.

105 Art. 1.5 septies and 1.6.f, Decreto Legislativo 58/1998.

106 Art. 2.3, Circulaire FMA du 4 mai 2005 sur l'analyse financière.

107 Art. 2 and 21, Loi n. 513/1991.

108 Loi du 25 avril 2014 relatif au statut et contrôle des planificateurs financiers indépendants et à la fourniture de consultations de planification financière and Décret royal du 8 juillet 2014 applying thereto.

109 FSMA Questions et réponses relatives à la planification financière, question n. 20 (as of 30 September 2015).

covered by CRD IV[110] and that European credit institutions can therefore avail themselves of the passport in order to exercise it, it must be recognised that financial planning services as described above do not fit easily into one of the activities listed in Annex 1 of said directive. Notwithstanding this question of interpretation, one should consider that promoting such services in Belgium or into Belgium is no longer possible for a UK firm.

Chapter 2: Authorisation aspects as regards financial products

2.1 Local private placement regimes

The AIFMD allows Member States to implement local authorisation (national private placement regimes, NPPR). However, these do not exist in all Member States as certain countries such as Germany have abolished their private placement arrangements. The use of an NPPR after Brexit may not be possible as these will disappear when third-country marketing passports are made available. It is likely the NPPRs will be abolished by 2019. Even if various NPPRs are available after Brexit or if there is a delay to Brexit they require analysis on a country by country basis in terms of flexibility and applicability. For UCITS, there are no (local) private placement regimes.

2.2 Product intervention at local level

Furthermore, as mentioned above, the national competent authorities have been given market and product intervention powers by MiFIR, the PRIIPs Regulation and the Short Selling Regulation alongside the ESAs. This includes the task of monitoring financial markets in the particular Member State. Although the intervention powers under MiFIR do not apply until 3 January 2018, some Member States have already introduced such powers for their national supervisory authority, for example, in Germany for the Federal Financial Supervisory Authority (BaFin) through the Retail Investors Protection Act of 3 July 2015. The exercise of powers by national supervisory authorities is only possible under certain conditions. The Member State in question must be affected and the problem cannot be solved by improved supervision. The intervention must not have a discriminatory effect on cross-border activities from other Member States. The supervisory authority must announce the intervention one month in advance and only in exceptional circumstances within 24 hours. The relevant ESA should ensure that the intervention of the national supervisory authority is justified and proportionate, as well as consistent with other national supervisory authorities, however, the national supervisory authority may act contrary to the ESA's opinion. Recently, local regulators in Poland[111], Germany[112], France[113], Belgium[114], Italy[115], Spain[116], Malta[117] and

---

110 FSMA Questions et réponses relatives à la planification financière, question n. 37 (as at 30 September 2015).

111 Office Statement of the Polish Financial Supervision Authority, DRK/WRM/485/55/1/55/2013/PT.

112 BaFin General Administrative Act (...) regarding contracts for difference (CFD) of 8 May 2017, Ref. no.: VBS 7-Wp 5427-2016/0017; BaFin Draft General Administrative Act (...) regarding credit-linked notes of 28 July 2016, VBS 7-Wp 5427-2016/0019, 2016/1332459.

Ireland[118] (as well as in the UK[119]) have issued warnings and considered or issued specific intervention measures covering the marketing and sale of products such as credit-linked notes, CfDs, binary options and contingent convertible bonds to retail investors.

Chapter 3: Tolerance thresholds for promotional activity

Each Member State determines the point from which promotional activity of a third-country firm requires a licence differently. The triggering event for licensing is specific to national regulation (3.1). Member States can also define specific safe harbours (3.2), have a different understanding of the concept of reverse solicitation (3.3) or offer cross-border licences (3.4).

3.1 Triggering event for licensing

Promotional activity generally involves different phases ranging from advertising, to first contact, the presentation of the firm and its services and the negotiation of agreements. It typically concludes with the signing of such agreements. When a UK firm acts in or towards Member States of the EU, it must understand to what extent it may undertake promotional and solicitation activity without a licence. For the reasons mentioned above, this tolerance threshold is defined in practice by national regulations and not by EU directives, most often through interpretative acts or decisions by regulators. There are thus currently 29 different approaches (including Gibraltar) in the EU.

i. *Advertising*

In a majority of Member States, local regulations make a distinction between generic marketing (brand awareness) and advertising of specific services and financial products. The latter type of advertising almost always results in a license requirement. On the other hand, this is not the case for generic advertising, which is treated differently from country to

---

113 AMF Q&A, Prohibition of promotional communications relating to the provision of investment services in respect of certain financial contracts, DOC-2017-01.

114 Guidelines of the FSMA n° 2015_08 of 27th July 2015 as regards contingent convertible debt instruments.

115 CONSOB Q&A of 23 June 2015 and CONSOB newsletter no. 50 of 29 December 2014, both on complex products – risks for retail investors.

116 CNMV press release of 21 March 2017 regarding measures on the marketing of CfDs and other regulated products to retail investors

117 MFSA Policy Document applicable to Online Business Models Distributing or Intending to Distribute Contracts for Difference (CFDs) and/or Rolling Spot Forex Contracts under the MiFID Regime, Online Forex 03.04.2017.

118 Central Bank of Ireland Consultation Paper 107 on the protection of retail investors in relation to the distribution of contracts for difference of 6 March 2017.

119 FCA, Temporary product intervention rules, Restrictions in relation to the retail distribution of contingent convertible instruments, 5 August 2014 ; FCA PS15/14 and CP14/23: Restrictions on the retail distribution of regulatory capital instruments ; FCA CP 16/40, Enhancing conduct of businessrules for firms providing contract for difference products to retail clients.

country[120]. In France, it is not considered, in itself, as an activity that requires prior licensing of a firm[121]. It is however recommended to act with caution as it is not easy to draw the limit between generic marketing and the promotion of services. Other regulators, like CONSOB in Italy, have a more extensive interpretation of brand promotion and are quick to consider that corporate advertising is an activity restricted to licensed firms[122]. Other countries, such as Poland, seem to go even further and consider that any generic publicity, even without a mention of any services, amounts to promotional activity that requires prior licensing.

Promotion via websites is also subject to a range of treatments. More precisely, the factors that lead regulators to consider that a website targets the general public in a particular country varies according to national practice. We note, however, that countries that have a specific national language, often focus on language as a connecting factor. Furthermore, supervisory authorities are starting to establish rules, differing from country to country, regarding marketing via social media (blogs, Twitter, Facebook etc.)[123].

ii. Approaching a prospect and presentation of the firm and its services

Simply meeting a potential client would not lead to financial services licensing requirements as long as such contact is just at a social level. Beyond such casual contact, most European countries have adopted a solicitation test, meaning that a foreign service provider would be subject to a licence requirement as soon as he starts to promote his firm or his services, on-site or from abroad[124]. Even if prospecting as such does not constitute an activity subject to licensing, it could be prohibited by other local rules[125]. There are also other Member States that have a more liberal approach and only require a licence where a contract is entered into or a service is provided in or towards a country. In Luxembourg, for example, it seems possible to engage in preliminary activity on an occasional basis whilst physically present in the country with a view to establishing a relationship or selling a service[126]. Promotional steps are also tolerated by the Spanish regulator regarding banking services only. The supervisory authority considers that the connecting factor is the place where a service is provided, i.e. where an account is opened and where the funds are accepted. Physical presence by a UK firm's representatives on Spanish territory should however only be on an occasional basis, lest it creates a factual branch. The Spanish approach is more restrictive regarding investment

---

[120] This is also referred to as "publicité de notoriété" (goodwill advertising), for example in Luxembourg: Chap. II.4.b, Circ. CSSF 11/515.

[121] Art. 341-2-11, Code monétaire et financier states that "the dissemination to natural or legal persons of simple advertising information, without any contractual or pre-contractual documents, whatever the medium used" is not a prospecting activity.

[122] See in particular: Communication CONSOB N. DIN/2049119 of 15 July 2002.

[123] For example in the UK: FCA FR 15/4 The FCA's supervisory approach to financial promotion on social media.

[124] For example Austria: Protocol signed between FINMA and the FMA on "market access rules" following the bilateral treaty known as Rubik of 1 January 2013 (Circ.- ASB 7762).

[125] For example in France the prospecting rules must be read in conjunction with those on the exercise of a financial activity (Art. L. 341-1, CMF).

[126] Chap. II.4.b, Circ. CSSF 11/515.

services subject to the supervision of another regulator. The Czech regulator also seems to consider that the prospecting phase does not yet constitute the exercise of an activity subject to a licence.

iii. Negotiation and signing of agreements

Certain Member States consider that the negotiation and signing, on national territory, of agreements regarding financial services constitutes, without exception, the undertaking of banking or investment services activity subject to authorisation. In France, the regulator considers that this would be an essential act included in the concept of a "body of evidence", which is referred to in order to determine whether or not there is financial services activity subject to a licence. The negotiation and signing of agreements within the country also seems to be subject to licensing in Slovakia. Dispatching or handing over contractual forms in Poland is considered by the Polish regulator to be an offer of regulated services and is thus subject to authorisation under local financial services law.

Certain Scandinavian countries, on the other hand, consider that the signing of contractual documents on their territory is permitted, if this results from a client's initiative. Regarding banking services, a UK firm can have an agreement signed in Spain even if this is the result of promotional activity, provided that presence in Spain is on an occasional basis.

3.2 Safe harbours

Most legal systems recognise, sometimes unofficially, certain practices that avoid the need for licensing. These privileged situations are referred to as *safe harbours*. Two examples are mentioned below:

i. Quantitative thresholds

Some legal systems consider that there is only a licensing requirement if the targeted activity exceeds a certain threshold of materiality. Belgium, for example, has set a material threshold of 50 persons to determine the point at which prospecting banking services is subject to a banking licence.[127] This limit does not appear in the Belgian regulations on investment services. Other countries, like Sweden also have a quantitative tolerance threshold, without however setting a numerical limit. Promotional activity therefore remains possible, even on-site, provided that visits only take place on an occasional basis and, on the whole, with a limited number of prospects.

[127] Art. 1, Arrêté royal du 9 octobre 2009 relatif au caractère public de la sollicitation de fonds remboursables.

ii. Status of client or prospect

The French legal system adopts a very strict approach resulting in a large number of rules covering financial services activity and related prospecting. However, these prescriptions do not apply if the prospect or the client is a professional within the meaning of the local definition based on MiFID II.[128] In this case, a UK firm could carry out prospecting activities, but only on a remote basis in order not to be subject to the rules on regulated activities.

Other Member States also provide operational opportunities based on the prospect's or the client's status, but by taking into account other definitions. Poland allows non-EU banks to prospect those persons who are professionals within the meaning of the local civil law i.e. natural or legal persons who exercise a professional activity for their own account[129]. The Dutch law allows offering banking services actively to *professional market participants* i.e. to persons whose assets exceed a certain threshold[130].

iii. Product placement

For financial products, national private placement regimes can signify a safe harbour. However, as mentioned above, there is a tendency to abolish such regimes at the local level for the sake of EU-wide harmonisation. The NPPRs for AIFs will disappear in due course and it will then be only the Prospectus Directive (art. 4) that will allow private placement of transferable securities under limited circumstances. As an example, at the national level, Germany only allows private placement of capital investments under equally narrow conditions[131].

A possible additional safe harbour for placing products is when this occurs under a discretionary asset management mandate as this is permitted in some Member States, e.g. in France.

iv. Reverse solicitation

Passive solicitation is also a safe harbour. Given its importance, it deserves detailed consideration.

a. Recognition by the EU

At the EU level, recognition of reverse solicitation as a factor obviating the need for licensing of financial service providers is not a general rule. The legal situation must be examined with regard to the directives on financial services.

---

128 Art. L. 341-2 and L 411-2, CMF.
129 Art. 43, Civil Code.
130 Art. 2:11 ff., Act on financial supervision.
131 § 2(1) sub-paragraph 3 Capital Investments Act (Gesetz über Vermögensanlagen, VermAnlG).

Regarding banking services, CRD IV does not mention reverse solicitation. Recognition comes however, indirectly, from the free movement of capital (art. 63 FEU Treaty). Third-country credit institutions may therefore respond to a client's opening request without being necessarily obliged to seek a licence from the Member State in which the prospect is resident, even if the latter's request is made from his country of residence.

Regarding investment activities, Article 42 of MiFID II and Article 46 MiFIR provide a firmer and more direct legal basis regarding the recognition of the client's initiative. If the service provider responds *"at the exclusive initiative"* of the client, he can act more often without to apply for a licence in the country being prospected. We emphasise that this legal provision excludes the concept of subsequent solicitation by the provider of any other categories of services or products.

Regarding mortgage loans, the Mortgage Credit Directive does not recognise reverse solicitation. The directive is therefore applicable even if the initiative comes from the client, if the residential property to be financed is located within the EU.

b. National recognition

With regard to prospecting activity, the principle of reverse solicitation is interpreted differently from country to country in the EU. For a UK firm, it is crucial to understand the particularities of each national interpretation. The differences mainly concern the following points:

- *Geographical scope*. Here we have two competing interpretations. Some regulators consider that third-country banks, upon a prospect's request, can present their services and provide documentation on a remote basis and when physically present. Other regulators, on the other hand, consider that passive solicitation only allows banks to act on a remote basis from the service provider's country of incorporation. Currently, it is considered that the attitude of the Belgian legislator is restrictive regarding this point and that it is preferable, even upon client request, not to engage in any promotional activity on Belgian territory. This is also the case in France. Other countries, on the contrary, allow foreign banks to prospect on-site on a passive basis, in particular Austria[132], Romania and Finland. The situation remains unclear in certain other countries such as Italy.
- *Conceptual scope*. Here there are also two tendencies. Some Member States have a very restrictive, even limitative, understanding of reverse solicitation. The prospect must clearly express his request and the service provider cannot go beyond this initial request. In addition, the initiative must not be in any way induced by any prior steps of the third-country firm. Belgium and Italy clearly belong to this category. On the

[132] Protocol signed between FINMA and the FMA on "market access rules" following the bilateral treaty known as "Rubik" of 1 January 2013 (Circ.- ASB 7762).

other hand, there are Member States that have a broader understanding of a client initiative. Once a client expresses his wish to be informed, anything is possible.

- Temporal scope. The client's request can also have an effect over time and last throughout the business relationship. In Austria and Germany[133], signing an initial document is recognised as the basis of reverse solicitation for the whole duration of the relationship. Other Member States only consider a passive request as an ad hoc request on a time limited basis.

One cannot exclude that the EU regulators will one day fully define the concept of reverse solicitation and thus reduce the different interpretations between Member States and in fact this seems probable following implementation of the MiFID II package. Regarding passive solicitation related to financial products, ESMA has already started to address the issue in a recent written opinion.[134]

v. Cross-border licences

When a licence is necessary in order to promote activities performed in or towards a country of the EU, i.e. for activity with retail clients under MiFID II, it is usually a matter of obtaining authorisation to open a branch. A third country branch established in an EU-country is not entitled to a passport. Any prospecting by this branch towards other Member States is therefore subject to the same restrictions that apply to a bank prospecting directly from outside of the EU.

There are fortunately some European countries whose legislation provides for cross-border licences. These facilitate the activity of prospecting and establishing business relationships and avoid having to create a branch. There are a limited number of EU Member States that offer this possibility and developments will need to be monitored following Brexit to see what approach is adopted towards the UK which will be dependent on any agreements made between the EU and UK. They are mentioned below in order of operational practicality afforded by the licence:

- *Germany*. Third country firms may utilise a type of cross-border licence called a *Freistellung*. This is based on a note by BaFin dated 2005[135], and requires the presence of a German (or an EEA) credit institution for establishing a relationship and that the beneficiary of this exemption complies with the German rules on investor protection. Note that Swiss entities have another type of *Freistellung* available based on an

133 Protocol signed between FINMA and the FMA on "market access rules" following the bilateral treaty known as Rubik of 1 January 2013 (Circ.- ASB 7762).

134 ESMA's opinion to the European Parliament, Council and Commission and responses to the call for evidence on the functioning of the AIFMD EU passport and the National Private Placement Regimes of 30 July 2015, nm. 228 (ESMA/2015/1235).

135 BaFin, Merkblatt – Hinweise zur Erlaubnispflicht nach § 32 Abs. 1 KWG in Verbindung mit § 1 Abs. 1 und Abs. 1a KWG von grenzüberschreitend betriebenen Bankgeschäften und/oder grenzüberschretend erbrachten Finanzdienstleistungen, 1 April 2005.

exchange of letters between Switzerland and Germany and a performance agreement concluded between FINMA and the German regulator which entered into force on January 1, 2014. Under this Swiss/German arrangements direct promotional activity regarding private clients is possible. These *Freistellung* cover both banking and investment services. It therefore an ideal instrument in order to penetrate the German market, where any active prospecting from Switzerland is otherwise prohibited.

- *Italy*. This Member State also offers third-country service providers subject to appropriate supervision the possibility to obtain a cross-border licence, called *Libera prestazione di servizi* (LPS). The bank law authorises third-country banks to perform both banking and investment services in Italy without establishing a branch[136]. Cooperation agreements between third country regulators and the Bank of Italy and/or CONSOB are required. In practice, CONSOB is less and less willing to grant this kind of licence to non-EEA service providers.
- *Luxembourg*. In this Member State, it is also possible for a third country firm to apply for a cross-border licence, thus significantly improving the possibility of accessing the local market and, above all, of providing financial services on-site[137]. The licence covers all financial services, independently of a client's status.
- *Denmark*. Danish legislation also allows third-country service providers to apply for a cross-border licence. Despite the terminology used in the law (in its unofficial English version), which only mentions investment services, it is possible to consider that the Danish licence also covers banking services, including credit activities[138]. Promotion of financial services in Denmark is also possible under the licence.
- *Spain*. Here there are two cross-border licences, one for credit institutions, covering both banking services[139] and investment services[140], and the other one for providers of investment services, covering only investment services. The licences are granted by different authorities, who can make the exercise of these activities subject to specific conditions whose scope is as yet unclear.
- *Finland*. Local legislation provides for a cross-border licence only for investment services[141], allowing non-EU financial intermediaries to offer such services to any category of client.

---

136 Art.16(4), Testo unico bancario, 1 September 1993 (status as at 12 May 2015).

137 Chap. II.4.b, Circ. CSSF 11/515.

138 The legal basis is provided by Art. 33(4), Financial Business Act, 8 August 2011 (Consolidated Act n. 885). The scope of the licence is specified in the Executive Order n. 979 of 4 December 2003 and which, in order to define the services covered by the licence, refers to the services listed in the Annexes 2 to 4 of the law.

139 The licence is provided for in Art. 13(2), Ley 10/2014, dated 26 June, de ordenacion, supervision y solvencia de entitades de credito. The conditions are described in Art. 17(3), Real Decreto 84/2015 of 13 February, pr el que se desarrolla la Ley 10/2014.

140 The licence is provided for in Art. 71 quarter, Ley 24/1988 dated 28 July, del Mercado de valores. The conditions are described in Art. 54, Real Decreto 217/2008, dated 15 February, sobre el regimen juridico de la impresas de servicio de inversion.

141 Chap. 5, Sect. 5 of the Finnish Act on Investment Services (747/2012). Only the creation of a branch is possible for banking services (Chap. 17 of the Finnish Act on Credit Institutions (610/2014).

- *Belgium.* The cross-border licence provided for by Belgian legislation[142] only covers investment services and only authorises promotional activity by non-EEA firms towards institutional clients or towards nationals of the non-EEA firm's country resident in Belgium. Given its limited scope, it has not been an efficient solution in the past for Swiss firms and the same is likely to be the case for UK firms.

It is also worth mentioning the Netherlands and Hungary, which have an exemption system regarding the offer of investment services and credits, respectively. As regards the Netherlands it should be noted that the regulator is in the process of reconsideration of the scope of this exemption regime which for the time being is only granted to the USA, Australia and Switzerland.

Finally, we point out the case of Greece, which in 2014 revoked the legal provisions that allowed a third-country firm to obtain a cross-border licence[143]. The Greek authorities seem to have considered that the system of cross-border licences is not compatible with the new CRD IV Directive. We are of the opinion that this is not the case and that the Greek decision goes against the commitments made by this country under the OECD Code of Liberalisation of Capital Movements and of Current Invisible Operations.

[142] Art. 25 ff, Arrêté royal du 20 décembre 1995 relatif aux entreprises d'investissement étrangères.

[143] Art. 36, Law 4261/2014 on the access to the activity of credit institutions and prudential supervision of credit institutions and investment firms (transposition of Directive 2013/36 EU), which revokes Law 3601/2007.

Conclusion

The conclusion that one can draw from the above analysis is that prospecting and establishing business relationships in EU Member States is certainly subject to significant limitative constraints resulting from EU law, but that to date the scope of these obstacles depend, to a large extent, on the national regulation of each Member State. UK firms that intend to prospect in the EU must therefore have a country-by-country approach and adapt their operating model to reality on the ground which will of course depend on different national interpretations of EU law and regulation.

The UK will become a third country with respect to the EU and so prima facie should be able to use the various mechanisms available which give limited access to EU clients and markets under EU legislation, e.g. MiFID II/MiFIR, AIFMD, etc. Bearing in mind the fragmented and piecemeal approach to third-country access, negotiations between the UK and EU will likely result in changes to the current framework for equivalence and third-country access, as this is an objective of both sides. Readers of this paper will need to monitor developments as they occur.